Cambridge checkp●int

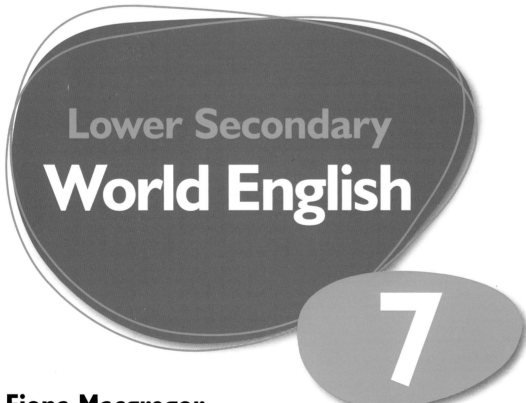

Lower Secondary
World English

7

Fiona Macgregor
Daphne Paizee
EDUCATIONAL CONSULTANT:
Sioban Parker

HODDER
EDUCATION
AN HACHETTE UK COMPANY

Registered Cambridge International Schools benefit from high-quality programmes, assessments and a wide range of support so that teachers can effectively deliver Cambridge Lower Secondary. Visit www.cambridgeinternational.org/lowersecondary to find out more.

Cambridge International copyright material in this publication is reproduced under licence and remains the intellectual property of Cambridge Assessment International Education.

The tests and mark schemes/answers have been written by the authors. These may not fully reflect the approach of Cambridge Assessment International Education.

Third-party websites and resources referred to in this publication have not been endorsed by Cambridge Assessment International Education.

The authors would like to thank Susan Kelly for her excellent input and guidance while developing this material, and Rebecca Norman for her diligent and conscientious editing.

The audio files are free to download at www.hoddereducation.com/cambridgeextras

Although every effort has been made to ensure that website addresses are correct at time of going to press, Hodder Education cannot be held responsible for the content of any website mentioned in this book. It is sometimes possible to find a relocated web page by typing in the address of the home page for a website in the URL window of your browser.

Hachette UK's policy is to use papers that are natural, renewable and recyclable products and made from wood grown in well-managed forests and other controlled sources. The logging and manufacturing processes are expected to conform to the environmental regulations of the country of origin.

Orders: please contact Hachette UK Distribution, Hely Hutchinson Centre, Milton Road, Didcot, Oxfordshire OX11 7HH. Telephone: +44 (0)1235 827827. Email: education@hachette.co.uk Lines are open from 9 a.m. to 5 p.m., Monday to Friday. You can also order through our website: www.hoddereducation.com

ISBN: 978 1 3983 1141 1

© Daphne Paizee and Fiona Macgregor 2021

First published in 2021 by
Hodder Education
An Hachette UK Company
Carmelite House
50 Victoria Embankment
London EC4Y 0DZ
www.hoddereducation.com

Impression number   10 9 8 7 6 5 4 3 2 1
Year   2025 2024 2023 2022 2021

Cover © kalafoto - stock.adobe.com

Typeset in FS Albert 12/14pt by Ian Foulis Design, Saltash, Cornwall

Printed in Italy

A catalogue record for this title is available from the British Library.

Contents

Introduction

How can English help you in your everyday life and connect you to the exciting and challenging world in which we live? In *Cambridge Checkpoint Lower Secondary World English* we encourage you to connect to this world by thinking and reflecting as you learn.

We have provided topics for a variety of different interests, from living in remote areas to using social media and making business plans. You will have the opportunity to use the new language that you learn to share ideas and learn from others too. This will help you to become confident and fluent in English. The language and the skills that you learn will also help you in other subjects.

Cambridge Checkpoint Lower Secondary World English therefore helps you to access your world and to stay connected to it. Be the best that you can and become a responsible and thinking citizen of the world.

Enjoy your learning experience!

Daphne Paizee
Fiona Macgregor

How to use this book

To make your study of Cambridge Lower Secondary English as a Second Language as rewarding as possible, look out for the following features when you are using this book.

- These aims show you what you will be covering in the unit.

PRACTISE
Activities that help you to put new skills, information and knowledge to practical use.

Try this

These questions help you to develop skills, knowledge and comprehension.

CHALLENGE YOURSELF
These are more demanding tasks or tasks that help you to practise a wider range of skills.

Do you remember?

These provide a quick recap on earlier grammar points and may sometimes include a question.

LET'S TALK
These tasks provide opportunities for more free discussion.

DID YOU KNOW?
These contain interesting information or facts.

HINT
Useful points to note or help with an activity.

Self check
Summary questions or tasks that occur at the end of each unit.

What can you do?

This provides an end-of-unit checklist of key content.

This book contains lots of activities to help you learn. Most of these have symbols beside them to help you know what type of activity they are.

This means that there is a listening activity, along with an audio track reference. All audio is available to download for free from www.hoddereducation.com/cambridgeextras

This means that there is a speaking activity. These are different to the Let's Talk boxes, which are freer discussion tasks that usually occur towards the end of a unit.

This tells you that content is related to another subject.

There is a link to digital content at the end of each unit if you are using the Boost eBook.

At the end of this book you will find some additional features to help you while you study.

- The glossary is a list of some words you might not have encountered before, or words that are specific to one of the units you will be studying. If you want to check the meaning of a word you come across in this book, check the glossary. If it's not there, use a dictionary.
- The grammar section includes all the grammar points you will learn throughout this book. It is arranged in alphabetical order so you can find everything easily.
- Check the punctuation chart to remind yourself how to use punctuation accurately in your own writing. This chart will help you understand different forms of punctuation and how to use them properly.
- The pronunciation word bank is a list of interesting words that appear in this book. You might not have heard some of these words before. Listen to the Audio list of these words to learn to pronounce them properly. Read the words as you listen.
- At the back of the book is a list of books you might like to read for enjoyment. Reading is a great way to relax, to use your imagination, and to learn about new people, places and things. Most of all – it's fun!

1 Friends

In this unit you will:
- listen to a poem about friends, and conversations between friends
- listen to a podcast about making friends in a **community**
- talk about and describe friends and friendship
- read journal entries and a magazine article about making friends
- write tips about how to make friends
- use different present tense verbs and pronouns in your speaking and writing.

Speaking and listening

My friends

Listen to the poem in Audio 1.1 and read it as you listen.

My friends

My friends are …
Fabulous
Respectful
Important
Extraordinary
Non-judgemental
Dependable
SPECIAL!

> **DID YOU KNOW?**
> You may notice that the letters at the beginning of the words in the poem make up the word FRIENDS. This is called an acrostic poem.

> **LET'S TALK**
> Do you agree with the description in the poem? Which of the words would you use to describe your friends? Can you think of other words to describe your friends? Discuss this with a partner and then share your ideas with the **class**.

Try this

Listen carefully to these words in Audio 1.2 as you read them in the table below. Check that you know what each word means. If you are not sure what a word means, how can you find out?

F	R	I	E	N	D	S
funny	reliable	interesting	easy-going	nice	dear	supportive
forgiving	real	informal	encouraging	non-judgemental	disciplined	sweet
fantastic	respectful	impressive	earnest	needed	diligent	sincere
				nearby	direct	

PRACTISE

1 Work in pairs or on your own. Choose words beginning with F, R, I, E, N, D and S and make up your own acrostic poem. Write your poem in your notebook. Be sure to spell all the words correctly!

2 Read your poem aloud.

Speaking and listening

Understanding conversations

1   Now you will hear students greeting each other on the first day of school. Listen to the first conversation in Audio 1.3.
    ● What are the students talking about?
    ● How do they greet each other?
    ● Do you greet your friends in the same way?
    ● Do they know each other?

> PRACTISE
>
> Work in groups. Role-play how you greet your friends at the beginning of the school year, after not seeing each other over the holidays.

2   Now listen to the conversation in Audio 1.4.
    ● Who is new at the school?
    ● What expressions do the students use?
    ● Is Malik friendly?

> PRACTISE
>
> Work in groups.
>
> 1   Role-play how you introduce yourself to a new student. Use ideas from the dialogue you listened to in Audio 1.4
> 2   Listen to the audio dialogues again. Listen to the intonation in the questions carefully. How do you need to change your voice at the end of a question? Try your role-play again and improve your intonation.

Describe a friend

Read these descriptions that students wrote of their friends.

This is my best friend Mara. She is American. She was born in California. She has long brown hair in braids and brown eyes and she is quite tall. She is fun! She laughs and smiles all the time. She is also caring, kind and generous. I don't know what I would do without her.

John is my best friend. He is the same age as me, but he is shorter. He has dark straight hair and braces on his teeth. He is called 'the thinker' because he is always thinking up new games. He is loyal and honest and very respectful of others. He can be very funny too.

Try this

Give a short description of one of your friends. You can use words from the poem that you made too.
- Say what your friend looks like.
- Say something about the kind of person your friend is.

PRACTISE

Let's play a game!

Get into groups of ten or more and play this guessing game.

One person will be the guesser. The guesser stands with his or her back to the board (or with closed eyes).

Another member of the group (or your teacher) writes the name of one student in the group on the board.

The others in the group then give the guesser clues about the person, without saying the name. The clues should describe the person. For example:
- She has long hair.
- He is always laughing.

GUESS WHO ?

Use of English

Present simple tense

As you may have noticed, you used the present simple tense to describe your friends in the earlier activities. We use the present simple tense:

- to talk about habits and routines
- to describe people
- to talk about things that are always true.

For example:

I/We/You/They have short, curly hair.

She/He wears glasses. (The verb for the third person singular ends in -s.)

I/We/You/They don't wear glasses.

He/She doesn't have many friends.

There is more on the present simple tense in the grammar support section at the end of this book.

PRACTISE

Which verb is correct? Read the sentences aloud to a partner and choose the correct verb.

1 My friend (have/has) very short hair.
2 The girls (play/plays) football.
3 We often (go/goes) to the gym.
4 She (don't/doesn't) have any friends.
5 They (don't/doesn't) have time to go to the shop.

Try this

Write these sentences using the correct form of the present simple tense.
1 He (to have) long brown hair.
2 She (to wear) glasses.
3 They (to be) all 13 years old.
4 Marik (to go) to the gym every day.
5 Jodi and Mara (to play) a lot of football.

Do you remember?

Think about the way you asked questions in your role-plays. Which words did you use? There are different ways of asking questions. Look at these examples and discuss how the questions are formed. What rules do you know about this?

For example:

Do you have brothers and sisters?

Does she/he have many friends?

Where do you live?

Were you born here?

You aren't from here, are you?

Shall we go?

CHALLENGE YOURSELF

Work in groups. Take it in turns to ask each person in the group three questions about themselves. Try to ask different types of questions.

There is more information on asking questions in the grammar section at the end of this book.

Try this

Work in pairs. Complete the questions in this conversation. Use the simple present tense where possible.

Jon: Hello. My name is Jon. _____ you in my class?

Sabine: Yes, I am. I'm Sabine.

Jon: Sabine, can you tell me _____ is the science lab? And _____ are the toilets?

Sabine: You're new at this school, _____ you?

Jon: Yes, I am! And I'm lost.

Sabine: Don't worry. _____ I show you around?

Jon: Yes, please!

Sabine: _____ are you from?

Jon: I am from the Netherlands. From Amsterdam.

Sabine: Oh wow! _____ you born there?

Jon: Yes. _____ are you from?

Sabine: I am from Germany.

Reading

Read journals

1 Look at the photograph. This girl is at a new school and it is the first week. How do you think she feels? Choose words from the box to describe how she feels.

lonely	friendless
alone	popular
lost	**outcast**
happy	by herself
sad	together
excited	

2 Now read these two journal entries. Both entries were written by a girl called Mary during her first week at a new school.

Tuesday

New year, new school … new friends???

My new school is so big. And there are many classes. I feel lost. Where do I go??? Everyone else seems to know where to go.

But the other girls and boys are friendly. They all say 'Hiya' which means 'Hi' I suppose. Do they all know each other already? Are they all friends?

I am alone at break every day, but that's fine. I like being alone. But it's also a bit lonely. How do I make new friends? Do I just go up and say, 'Hello. I'm Mary. I want to be your friend?' That sounds silly. Do I share my lunch? Not sure what to do.

Friday

I have a new friend — I think? Her name is Alice. She is very funny! I like her. Hope we will be friends. We live in the same apartment block so we can walk to school together. She has a brother and a sister at the same school. She was born in Australia too. She is named after her grandmother, and I'm also named after my grandmother. What a coincidence!

3 Ask and answer these questions with a partner.
   a How does Mary feel on Tuesday?
   b How do others greet her?
   c Is she lonely?
   d How does she feel on Friday?
   e What is her new friend's name?
   f Where do they live?
   g Where was Alice born?
   h Are Alice and Mary named after their mothers or their grandmothers?

Try this

Read Mary's journal for Tuesday again. Give Mary some advice about how to make friends.

Start like this: You could _____.

Spelling

1 Learn to spell these words. Notice how they all end with the same letter.

very	friendly	already	many	funny	every

2 Work in pairs. Use the words in the box to complete these sentences.
   a She is new but she _____ has many new friends.
   b This is such a _____ school! Everyone greets you.
   c There are _____ new students at the school this year.
   d I say hello to my friends _____ day.
   e He has a _____ cool pair of shades.
   f I read a _____ story on **social media** yesterday. It made me laugh.

CHALLENGE YOURSELF

Do you remember your first day at a new school or in a new place? How did you feel? Write a short journal entry about this. Use the present tense and some of the words you practised for spelling. Share your writing if you want to.

Use of English

Pronouns

Do you remember?

Can you identify all the pronouns in the following sentences?

1   This is my friend Mara. She is called Super-Mara by her friends. She has long hair. I sit next to her in class. We enjoy ourselves.
2   Who is he? Is he your cousin?

Discuss why pronouns are useful and when we can use them.

PRACTISE

Work in pairs. Read the following sentences aloud and identify the pronouns.

1   How do I make new friends? Do I just go up and say, 'Hello. I'm Mary. I want to be your friend'?
2   I have a new friend – I think? Her name is Alice. She is named after her grandmother, just like me!

Try this

Read this dialogue aloud. Use pronouns instead of the underlined nouns.

> **Malik**: Hi Tyrone. Can <u>Tyrone</u> show <u>Malik</u> where the computer room is?
>
> **Tyrone**: Hiya. Of course <u>Tyrone</u> can. <u>The computer room</u> is next to the office, on the right.
>
> **Malik**: Thanks. Can <u>Malik and Tyrone</u> walk there together?
>
> **Tyrone**: Yes. Let <u>Tyrone</u> get <u>Tyrone's</u> books and <u>Malik and Tyrone</u> can go.

PRACTISE

Choose the correct pronoun to complete each sentence.

1   I have a new friend. (His/Her) name is David.
2   Who is that? Is she (you/your) new friend?
3   We need to prepare (myself/ourselves) for the new year at school.
4   We can help (each other/some other) with this project.
5   Where are my trainers? Has anyone seen (them/they)?
6   Look at all of these books. These are (my/mine). Are the other books (you/yours)?

Passive voice

Do you remember?

Look at the verbs in these two sentences:

I <u>was named</u> after my grandmother.

I <u>name</u> you Paul, after your grandfather.

- What is the difference?
  - Are they both in the same tense?
  - If not, what tense are they? Present or past?
- Are the verbs formed in the same way?
  - Does the auxiliary 'was' make a difference?
  - Which sentence is in the passive voice?

We can use the active voice or the passive voice to describe present actions. For example:

Active voice	Passive voice
They name him after his father.	He is named after his father.
They book the students into a new school.	The students are booked into a new school.

Work in pairs. Complete this sentence about how we form the passive: To form the passive voice, we use a form of the verb 'to _____' with the _____ participle.

2 Use the verb in each sentence in the present passive voice and say the sentence aloud.
   a I (name) after my mother.
   b He (call) 'the thinker' by his friends.
   c The students (call) to a meeting.
   d They (sign up) at the football club.
   e The concert (enjoy) by all our parents and friends.
   f The meal (share) between the friends.

Reading

Read a magazine article

Before you read the magazine article, read the title of the article, look at the text in speech marks (' and ') and look at the pictures. What do you think the article is about?

Now read the first paragraph. Did the paragraph confirm what you predicted?

Making new friends

It's not always easy to make new friends. Some people are quite good at this – and they make it look easy, but most of us have to make an **effort**. It's not easy, because we feel shy or we may feel afraid that other people may not like us. We fear that we will be **rejected** by others, and that is **tough** to deal with. No one wants to feel rejected. It makes you feel as if you are not good enough.

'I think it's a good idea to join a club to meet new friends. My brother and I are members of the sports club. We both like to swim. Now we are in the club swimming team and we do lots of things with the team. It's a good place to meet people who enjoy the same things. We have lots of things **in common** – and it's healthy too.' – Rami.

We asked a few students to give us their tips for making friends. Here's what some of them said.

'I like to be alone sometimes so that I can read or knit. But when I feel lonely and I need to be with other people, I go out on my skateboard. I talk to people at the skate park about different tricks. I met my friend Mark that way. We both like skateboarding and now we often meet up.' – Bella

'I like people who study and who want to get ahead. So for me, the library is a good place to meet people. I often go there. The people I meet are like me. They work hard and they are ambitious. Sometimes people come up to me and introduce themselves, but I have to make an effort too. I have learned to go up to people and introduce myself!' – Lebohang

'I **chat online** sometimes, which is **interesting** but a bit impersonal. I prefer to talk face to face with people. I also only talk to people online if I already know them. Sometimes I go to the Buddy Bench in the park and I sit there. Someone always sits down next to me for a **chat**. Sometimes we chat for a long time. If I don't like the person, I just get up and say good-bye.' – Mano

 1 Discuss and answer these questions.
   a Who goes to the library to make new friends?
   b Where did Rami go to make friends?
   c Where is the Buddy Bench that Mano goes to?
   d Which of these ideas could you use to make friends?

2 Find the answers to these questions in the magazine article. Write your answers in your notebook.
   a Where does Lebohang go to meet new friends?
   b Which of these places, according to the ideas in this article, is a good place to meet friends? Circle all those that are correct.

library	post office	club	park

   c True or false: Bella likes to be alone sometimes.
   d Complete the sentence: When Bella feels lonely, she

   _____.

   e What happens when Mano sits down on the Buddy Bench?
   f Why did Rami and his brother join a sports club?
   g Why, in Lebohang's opinion, is the library a good place to make friends?
   h What is your **opinion**? Where is the best place to make friends? Give a reason for your answer.

Vocabulary

1 Find words which have the same meanings as the following words and phrases in the magazine article. Write these in your notebooks.
   a friend
   b by yourself
   c talk
   d ideas
   e on the internet
   f want to be successful
   g difficult
   h in person
   i that we share/are the same

2 Complete these sentences with the words 'alone' or 'lonely' to show you understand the difference in meaning. Write the complete sentences in your notebooks.
   a I like it when everyone leaves the class and I am _____.
   b Many people feel _____ when they go to a new school and don't know anyone.
   c Sometimes I feel sad and _____ and then I need to phone my friends and chat.
   d I do not like to be _____ at home at night. It's a bit scary!

Try this

We use the verb 'to make' in many ways. Make sentences with these words + the verb 'to make'. Do you understand your sentences?
   ● friends
   ● an effort
   ● a bed
   ● a mistake
   ● money
   ● sure

CHALLENGE YOURSELF

Punctuation makes texts easier to read. Here are some tips from other students about making friends. Can you rewrite these in your notebook with the correct punctuation to make them easier to read?
   ● Find a shop that you like. go to the shop and talk to the other customers in the shop. They may like the same things as you do ... Andy
   ● Learn some small talk Small talk can be about the weather about school about an **event** in the news **headlines**. Paulo

Speaking and listening

Listen to a podcast

You are going to listen to Audio 1.5, which is a podcast on a community radio station.

1 Listen once and then choose the words to complete the sentence below to describe the main ideas in the podcast.

This podcast is about:

a how to use social media

b what to do if you are lonely

c why people live in big cities.

2 Now read the sentences below. Listen to the podcast again and complete the sentences. Use a dictionary to check your spelling if you are not sure. You can write the sentences in your notebook.

Many of us live in big towns or cities, full of people, but we are _____. What can we do about this?

You can go to places where people of your _____ hang out. Go there often. Take your book or phone with you if that makes you feel better. Say '_____' to a few people.

You can also join a _____. Sports clubs are good because you can _____ at the same time. You can be with other _____ and you don't have to _____ all the time!

Or you can _____ a community programme. For example, next _____ we have a **campaign** to clean up the _____ that runs through the town, which is full of rubbish.

---

3 Do you agree with Amelia's suggestions?

4 Have you tried any of these ideas already?

5 Which suggestion do you like the most? Write it down if you can. Use it for the activity that follows.

> **LET'S TALK**
> What do you think about the community podcast? Work in groups and share your views.

> **CHALLENGE YOURSELF**
> Work in groups. Write a short podcast script giving advice to others at your school who feel lonely.

Writing

Punctuation

Try this

Read this text aloud. It is about how to make friends.

> I think that real friends are people you know and can talk to face-to-face not just online the best way to make real friends is to go to a place where other people are doing what you like to do so if you enjoy art join an art class you can talk about art first and then afterwards you can make friends with others in the art class

Did you find this easy or difficult? Why? What could you do to make this easier to read? Copy the paragraph into your notebook and make it easier to read. Then try reading it aloud again.

You will find more support on basic punctuation at the end of this book.

PRACTISE

Punctuate these sentences correctly. You will need to add capital letters, full stops, commas and question marks.

1   I want to make new friends what should I do
2   it is difficult to walk up to people you don't know and start talking to them
3   who is that boy is he new here
4   I live at number 8 first avenue its not far from here
5   lee and jon are from singapore they are new at your school

Express your opinion

You are going to write some tips about making friends.

1   Work in groups. Discuss and make a list of ten ways in which you think that people of your age can make friends. Give your own opinions and try to give reasons as well. Make notes as you work. For example:

> I think we should spend more time talking face-to-face.
>
> Reasons:
> - You get to know people better.
> - You can see what people are really thinking.
> - You can use smiles to communicate if you can't find the right words.

I think people should join sports clubs.

Reasons:
- There are lots of different people in clubs.
- You will have things in common that you can talk about.
- You can be with other people, but you don't have to talk all the time.
- It is healthy.
- You get to know how people behave and what they are really like.

2 Now choose the five tips that you think are the best and give a reason why you think each tip will work well.
You can start like this:

TIP 1: _____

I think that this is a good tip because _____.

TIP 2: _____

This will work if you _____.

Self check

- Do you have five tips?
- Have you given your opinions about why each tip will work?
- Have you checked your punctuation: capital letters, full stops, commas and colons?

What can you do?

Read and review what you can do.
- I can talk, read and write about how to make friends.
- I can use the present simple tense to describe friends.
- I know the difference between the active and the passive voice and can make sentences in the passive.
- I can use pronouns when I speak and write.
- I can use punctuation when I write sentences and paragraphs.
- I can express opinions and give reasons for my opinions.

 Now you have completed Unit 1, you may like to try the Unit 1 online knowledge test if you are using the Boost eBook.

2 Celebrations

In this unit you will:
- listen to short talks and a podcast about celebrations around the world
- read about traditional and unusual celebrations
- write an email to a friend
- use the past simple tense and passive voice
- learn new idiomatic expressions
- use connective words to give explanations and reasons.

Speaking and listening

Talk about celebrations

 1 Work in pairs. Look at the photographs above. They show different traditional celebrations and festivals in different parts of the world. Read the captions on page 23 aloud and match them to the photographs.

Lighting candles at a **shrine** in Malaysia.

Young people at a music and colours celebration in Bulgaria.

Minstrels in their **costumes** in Cape Town after New Year.

A traditional meal (Iftar) after sunset during Ramadan in Egypt.

2 Then work in groups and describe the photographs in more detail.
   a What are the people doing?
   b Where are they?
   c What are they wearing?

Try this

1 Work in groups. Talk about the celebrations that you know or take part in.
   - Is there a **ceremony**?
   - Do you have a **parade**?
   - Do you light candles or pray?
   - Do you eat **special** food?
   - Do you wear costumes or masks or any other special clothing?
   - Is there music or dancing?

2 Draw up a table to describe four of these celebrations. You could do something like this:

Celebration	Place	What we do	Food	Music and dance
Easter	Greece	Go to church, **parade** around the church	Eat red eggs and soup to end our fast	Traditional songs and dances

3 Share your information with other groups. Take turns to do short presentations to the rest of the class or to another group.

PRACTISE

1 Look at these words. They all have more than one syllable. Listen to these words in Audio 2.1 and then repeat them. Take care to stress the syllable underlined.

co<u>s</u>tumes	pa<u>ra</u>de	cele<u>bra</u>tion	<u>fe</u>stival
tra<u>di</u>tional	<u>ce</u>remony	<u>flo</u>wers	<u>ske</u>letons

2 Now listen to the conversation about the Day of the Dead festival in Audio 2.1. Talk about what you have just heard. What else do you know about this festival?

▲ The Day of the Dead festival in Mexico

Speaking and listening

Listen to podcasts

All over the world, people attend different festivals every year. Some of these festivals are quite unusual!

1 Before you listen to Audio 2.2, look at the photographs below. The people in the photographs are part of an unusual festival in Canada. Are you familiar with it, or have you seen photographs of this before? These people have **frozen** hair which looks like a **sculpture**. How do you think that happened? Talk about your ideas first. Then listen to the audio and find out!

2 Work in pairs. Listen to Audio 2.2 again and complete the sentences about the hair-freezing festival. Use words from this box.

selfies	sculptures	water
wet	freezes	Canada

a The festival takes place in _____.
b People sit in the warm _____.
c They _____ their hair first in the warm water.
d Then they make _____ with their hair.
e The hair _____ after one minute.
f You take _____ of yourself and enter the competition!

3 In Spain every year there is an annual festival called La Tomatina. Look at the photographs below. What do you think happened at that festival? Talk about your ideas. Then listen to Audio 2.3, which is an account of the event by someone who took part in it.

4 Work in pairs. Listen to Audio 2.3 again and answer the questions.
   a In which country does La Tomatina take place?
   b At what time of the year is it?
   c What happens during the festival? Complete the sentences.
      i People throw _____.
      ii They slide around on _____.
      iii The trucks spray _____ to clean up.

 PRACTISE

 Listen carefully to Audio 2.4. Practise saying the sentences yourself with the correct intonation and stress. They are written here as well, to help you.

> The town is famous for its festivals.
>
> The celebrations take place every year.
>
> We are very excited about the event!
>
> I am very interested in traditional dances.

LET'S TALK

Work in groups. Tell your group about an interesting or unusual tradition, festival or celebration that you know about. Start like this:

The _____ takes place in _____.

It is a _____ that celebrates _____.

Use of English

Prepositions after adjectives

Prepositions are usually short words such as *with, in, of, at* that describe **location**, time and direction.

Sometimes we use prepositions after adjectives to make phrases with a special meaning. For example:

> I am happy with the mask I made for the festival. ✓
>
> I am happy of the mask I made for the festival. ✗ We do not say this.

Here are some more examples:

> Are you <u>afraid of</u> water?
>
> The place is <u>famous for</u> its hot springs.
>
> We're very <u>excited about</u> the flower festival.
>
> They were all <u>dressed in</u> white for the celebration.
>
> The students are <u>good at</u> dancing.
>
> The ground was <u>covered in</u> flowers.

PRACTISE

Read these sentences and questions aloud. Use prepositions to complete the sentences.

1 Are you happy _____ the shoes that you bought?
2 The dancers aren't afraid _____ jumping high in the air.
3 This city is famous _____ its music festival.
4 We were completely covered _____ tomatoes!
5 I am not accustomed _____ throwing tomatoes at other people!

Match the words in each column to make sentences. Do this orally first. Then write the sentences in your notebook. Underline the adjective and preposition that follows in each sentence.

What were they so excited	on traditional wrestling?
My sister is very interested	to my house.
Is Marc keen	at the tourists who mocked them.
The women were angry	from the celebrations in your country.
The celebrations are held in a stadium which is close	about?
Our celebrations are very different	at playing a musical instrument?
The streets are full	in traditional dancing.
Are you any good	of people singing and dancing.

Simple past tense (active)

We usually form the simple past tense with **-ed**.

For example:

play = played   dance = danced

Some past tense verbs have irregular past tense forms.

For example:

go = went   take = took

Look at the list of irregular past tense verbs on pages 162–63 if you are not sure.

PRACTISE

Work in pairs. Imagine that you went to the hair-freezing festival in Canada or the tomato festival in Spain. Tell your partner about what you did and what you saw there. Use the simple past tense.

CHALLENGE YOURSELF

1   Write a short report on a celebration or festival that you attended. It can be real or imagined, and any kind of celebration or festival. Use the simple past tense.
2   Read your report to the class or to your group.

Reading

Read a magazine article

Unusual festivals

Tomato throwing and hair-freezing are not the only unusual festivals around the world. Here are some others.

Unusual festivals around the world

Cheese rolling

Have you ever **chased** a wheel of cheese? Every May, some adults in Brockworth, UK, chase wheels of cheese down Cooper's Hill. As Cooper's Hill is **bumpy** and **steep**, this activity is quite dangerous. Therefore, some years ago, it was decided that only adults could take part. In May 2019, six people were injured during the festival. More than 4000 people came to watch this festival.

Carving radishes

Have you ever eaten radishes? In Mexico they are carved into animals, flowers and many other things for the Night of the Radishes festival. In Spanish this is called 'Noche de los Rábanos'. The festival is held every year on 23 December in a city called Oaxaca.

It is said that the festival started after farmers at the market started carving radishes to **attract** the attention of their customers. So in 1897 the festival was declared an official festival of the city of Oaxaca. It is very popular and attracts many contestants and visitors.

Large radishes are used, and prizes are awarded for the best carvings.

Try this

Read the magazine article again. Work in pairs and answer these questions.

1 Can you give each photograph in the article a title that explains what it shows?
2 Where and when does the cheese-rolling festival take place?
3 Why are young people not allowed to take part?
4 How did the Night of the Radishes festival begin?
5 Why do you think this festival is popular? Give a reason.

Vocabulary and spelling

1 Read all these words aloud. Write down the words that you do not know and find out what they mean.

aware	carved	costume	mime	sculpture
bizarre	chase	disturb	parade	steep
bumpy	ceremony	frozen	participant	

2 These words have meanings that are the same as or very similar to one of the words in the list in question 1. Find the word in the list that matches each one.

rough	strange, unusual
run after	procession

3 Learn to spell the words in question 1 so that you can use them in your own writing later.

4 Read the underlined expressions in these sentences. Work in pairs and discuss what you think they mean. Then check in your dictionary.
  a The farmers wanted to <u>attract the attention of</u> their customers.
  b Many people <u>took part in</u> the festival.
  c Have you ever chased <u>a wheel of cheese</u>?

HINT
Look up the key words (the nouns or the verbs) in your dictionary and you will find idiomatic expressions with these words.

CHALLENGE YOURSELF
Work with a partner and find out about another bizarre or interesting festival. Make notes about:
● where it happens
● when it happens
● why it happens
● who takes part in the activities.

Report back to the class.

Use of English

Passive voice

Do you remember?

We use the verb 'to be' and the past participle to form verbs in the passive. The passive can describe an action and does not say who or what did an action. For example:

> The cheese is chased down a hill.

> The area was covered in flowers for the festival.

Can you identify the tenses in the examples above? Are they present tense? Past tense? Remember that some past participles are irregular. For example:

> The celebrations were held in May. ('held' is the past participle of 'hold').

> Their hair was frozen by the cold air.

Look at the list of irregular participles on pages 162–63 if you are not sure.

Try this

Work in pairs. Identify the sentences in the passive voice in this paragraph. Do you know what the active form of each verb is?

> Some people came up with the idea of an underwater music festival to make others aware of the coral reefs off the coast of Florida in the USA. Have you heard of this before? The Underwater Music Festival was started more than 35 years ago. It was a great **success**! Music is played through speakers under the water. People are asked to dress up for the festival and to make interesting looking instruments.

PRACTISE

Work in pairs. Use the verbs in brackets in the passive form in each sentence. Use the present or past tenses as necessary.

1. During Ramadan, meals (eat) after sunset.
2. I (cover) in soft red tomato pulp during the festival yesterday.
3. It (decide) that only adults could take part in the event last year.
4. Many people (injure) during the festival.
5. Flowers (throw) on the ground during the ceremony.
6. Beautiful masks (wear) by all the people at the festival.
7. The festival (hold) every year on 23 December.

Connectives

Do you remember?

Connectives are words that link words, phrases, sentences and ideas.

We can use connectives when we explain reasons and give explanations.

Can you identify the connectives in these examples? Which ideas are they connecting? Make a list of the connectives and use them in your own writing later on.

1 The people are wearing costumes because it is festival time.
2 The coral reefs are in danger, therefore we need to protect them.
3 As the reefs are in danger, we need to protect them.
4 It was very cold and my hair was wet, so my hair froze!
5 We bought candles so that we could light them at the shrine.
6 In Greece there are many traditional meals, such as tzatziki (yoghurt and cucumber), roast lamb and stuffed tomatoes.

PRACTISE

Join the sentences using one of the connectives in the box.

such as	because	therefore	as	so	so that

1 We are dancing. It is the Spring festival.
2 We are fasting. We do not eat during the day.
3 Mara wanted to go to the festival. She bought a ticket.
4 Nadir and Malik went out in the street. They could see the parade.
5 The hill is steep and bumpy. There are often accidents.

CHALLENGE YOURSELF

Improve this paragraph by adding at least four connectives.

Last night we went to the Yanbu flower festival. My mother wanted to see the flowers. My little brother wanted to go. There were fun rides. We went off in the afternoon. I was quite amazed at the displays. The ground was covered in flowers. There were also birds and butterflies. We walked around for a long time. My dad took my brother for a ride on the little red bus. We were tired and hungry. We went and had supper. The **fireworks** started at 10:00. We waited. That was the best part!

Reading

Read a magazine article

1 Before you read, talk about New Year celebrations where you live.
- Do you celebrate New Year?
- At what time of the year do you celebrate?
- How do you celebrate?

2 Read the cards that family and friends sent to each other at New Year.
- Talk about what the messages mean.
- Do you send messages like this?
- What do you say in your messages?

3 Read the title of the article below and look at the photographs. Say in one or two sentences what you think the article is about.

Happy New Year!
Always welcome the new morning with a new spirit, a smile on your face, love in your heart and good thoughts in your mind.

Say Hello to a New Year
Let's get it right this year

Out with the old and in with the new

Did you celebrate New Year last week? Did you celebrate the end of one year and the start of a new year? Many people celebrate a new year as it gives us the chance of a fresh start and an opportunity 'to get things right'.

The new year is celebrated in different ways and at different times of the year because some people use different calendars. In some countries, such as the United Kingdom and the United States, the new year is always celebrated on 1 January. In other countries, for example Korea, New Year celebrations (called Seollai) fall on different days each year. So in 2020, Koreans celebrated on 25 January, while in 2021 they celebrated on 12 February.

As always, for people who celebrated the new year on 1 January, the time of the celebrations was different because we live in different **time zones**.

New Year was celebrated in Australia and Malaysia before it was celebrated in London. And people in London celebrated before people in New York.

Here are some reports about the January New Year celebrations around the world.

Times Square in New York, USA, is famous for its New Year celebrations. This year it was estimated that about a million people joined in the celebrations. Millions more watched the event on television. At 12 seconds before midnight on 31 December, the count down to the new year began: 12, 11, 10, 9 ... as people counted down to midnight, a ball dropped down on a **flagpole** above Times Square. Then at midnight, it rained **confetti** in the square. Some of the confetti had messages of hope. A big clean-up was needed afterwards!

In Japan, people also celebrated the end of the year on 31 December. This is called Omisoka. People got together before midnight to eat bowls of toshikoshi **noodles**. Then at midnight they visited shrines and temples. They prayed for their families. Bells rang in the temples so that all the problems of the last year could be left behind.

On the Copacabana Beach in Brazil, people jumped into the **waves** in the sea so that they could wash away all the problems of the previous year. Then they watched a display of fireworks. Many people were dressed in white because that is the colour of peace. Many also went out afterwards for a traditional bowl of lentils. People say that lentils look like small coins, so if you eat lentils you will have money all year around in the new year!

4 Write your answers to these questions in your notebook.

   a In which month does a new year begin in many countries?

   b Why is a new year celebrated at different times in other countries?

   c True or false?

     ● In Times Square people dressed in white to celebrate New Year.

     ● People in Japan went to shrines and temples to pray at New Year.

   d Name two things that people in Brazil do to celebrate New Year.

   e Why do many people celebrate the new year? Give one reason.

   f Should we celebrate New Year? What do you think? Give a reason for your answer.

Vocabulary and spelling

1 Find words in the text that have the following meaning:

   a to wear clothes

   b small bits of paper that are thrown during a celebration

   c a pole on which you can hang a flag

   d a place where people go to worship (pray).

2 Practise spelling these words.

temple	shrine	religious	different	country	traditional

Idiomatic language

1 Work in pairs. Reread the article about New Year celebrations and discuss what the following expressions mean. You can look up the key words in a dictionary. Then read the sentence in which the expression was used. Does this context help you understand the meaning?

   a get it right

   b a fresh start

   c out with the old, in with the new

   d to count down

   e it rained confetti

2 Write a sentence to explain what each expression in question 1 means. Then share and discuss your ideas with the class.

CHALLENGE YOURSELF

Compile a short table to compare different ways in which people celebrate New Year around the world. Give your table headings, such as 'Reason for festival', 'Special clothes worn' and 'Foods eaten'. What similarities do you notice between the ways different people celebrate? What differences are there?

Do you remember?

Idioms are expressions with special meanings. When we use words together, we can create idiomatic expressions with meanings that are not the same as the individual words.

Speaking and listening

Listen to a text and work out the meaning

1 Listen to the short talk about the Chinese New Year celebrations in Audio 2.5. Read the sentences below. Then listen to the audio again and this time complete the sentences below. Copy them into your notebook and fill in the gaps.

> In 2020 the Chinese New Year started on _____. 2020 was the Year of the _____. The Chinese New Year begins when the new _____ is seen in the sky in January or February each year. Chinese families _____ and _____ their homes for New Year. Then families get together for a traditional _____. One of the traditional New Year foods is _____.

2 Work in pairs. Listen to the text again and work out what the following words and expressions mean. Discuss the meanings with a partner.
   a a lunar calendar
   b bad luck
   c to get rid of
   d decorations

Research and give a short talk

Work in pairs. You are going to give a short talk on an interesting festival or celebration that you have heard or read about. Reread some of the texts in this unit and look again at the research you did earlier on.

HINT

Record your draft talk and listen to yourself. Can you understand everything that you said? What can you do to make the talk clearer?

HINT

Use this checklist to make sure you have completed the task correctly.
- Does the first sentence capture attention?
- Did you describe where and when the celebration took place?
- Did you use the correct verb tenses?
- Have you used connectives?
- Is the talk two minutes long?

CHALLENGE YOURSELF

Decide on your topic → Do your research → Draft a short talk → Edit your talk → Do your presentation in pairs

- **Research:** Make short notes to answer these questions as you do your research:
  – What is the festival or celebration?
  – Where does it take place?
  – When does it take place?
  – What do people do during the festival or celebration?
- Draft: Read it aloud to your partner.
- Time yourself. The talk should take about two minutes. Make sure you know how to pronounce all the words you use.

Writing

Write an email

1 Many people have holidays around the time of their New Year celebrations. Read the following email about such a holiday. Look up any words that you do not understand.

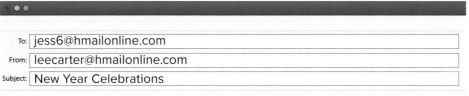

To: jess6@hmailonline.com

From: leecarter@hmailonline.com

Subject: New Year Celebrations

Date: 6 January

Hi Jess

Happy New Year! I hope it will be a happy and peaceful year for you and your family.

We started our year with an extra-big family celebration here in Cape Town. My cousins from the UK and from Italy came to visit. The house was full, but it was such fun!

On the day before New Year we took our cousins up Table Mountain and then we went for a swim in the sea. It's so hot here, much warmer than where you are. Then we all went home and had supper. That night we went down to the Waterfront to watch the firework display. It was amazing! We took selfies and sent pictures to other cousins and friends in the UK too. (We celebrated before them as they are in a different time zone!)

On New Year's Day we had a picnic lunch in Kirstenbosch Gardens. Then we went for a walk along the 'Boomslang', which is a walkway up through the trees – here is a photograph of the walkway.

We were all a bit tired. I fell asleep on the grass!

Now the holidays are nearly over, and it is almost time to go back to school.

Let me know what you have been doing.

Lots of love

Lee

2 Work in pairs. Look at the format of the email and find the following information.
  - The subject of the email.
  - The email address of the person who wrote the email.
  - The email address of the person to whom the email is written.
  - The greetings used to start and end the email.

3 Now plan, draft, edit and write a short email to a friend. Tell your friend about a celebration that you enjoyed. Include three paragraphs. Use the simple past tense and connectives to link your ideas.

HINT
- Draft your email and give it to a friend to read. Let your friend suggest how you can improve it. For example, is the punctuation correct? Are the verbs correct (in the simple past tense where necessary)?
- If you write your email on a computer, do not forget to use the spellcheck to check your work.

CHALLENGE YOURSELF
Write a reply to Lee's email that you read on page 36.

Self check
- Did you link ideas and sentences with connectives?
- Did you check the spelling of verbs with irregular past forms?
- Are your email addresses correct?

What can you do?

Read and review what you can do.
- I can listen to short talks and a podcast about celebrations around the world.
- I can read about traditional and unusual celebrations.
- I can write an email to a friend.
- I can use the past simple tense and passive voice.
- I can write new idiomatic expressions.
- I can use connective words to give explanations and reasons.

 Now you have completed Unit 2, you may like to try the Unit 2 online knowledge test if you are using the Boost eBook.

In this unit you will:
- listen to a song, a poem, a talk show programme about a recycling company and a programme about **waste** dumping
- discuss newspaper articles and posters and give your own opinion
- listen to arguments and the opinions of others
- talk about recycling, and have a debate about whose responsibility it is to get rid of waste
- read poems, newspaper articles and posters
- write a waste diary for a week and a blog about zero food waste
- use 'if' clauses in zero and first conditional, as well as the present continuous tense and adverbs.

Speaking and listening

What is waste?

 Look at the photographs above. Discuss these questions in your group.

Photograph 1:
- What is happening in this photograph?
- What else could you do with leftover food?

Photograph 2:
- Where do you think the pile of rubbish is?
- Can you describe how the rubbish ended up where it is?

Photograph 3:
- What does the green sign mean?
- Where have you see this sign before?
- Compare your ideas with those in your group.

Photograph 4:
- How many plastic bottles do you use at home every day?
- Can you think of some new uses for old plastic bottles?

Try this

Work with a partner. Match the captions to the pictures on the opposite page.

Did you know that not all plastic bottles can be recycled?
Recycle!
Most of our waste, or rubbish, ends up in places called **landfills**.
Too much food is **wasted** every day.

Vocabulary

How many words associated with the topic of 'waste' can you think of?

 1 Listen to this poem about waste in Audio 3.1. Read the words as you listen. Then read the poem out loud to your friend.

'Waste'

Bottles, bags, plastic and tins   Plant a herb in an old can
Put them all in separate bins   Use a bottle; make a plan
Don't just throw something away   There's so much that we all can do
Can it be used another way?   To clean our planet; me and you.

2 Write down the rhyming words from the poem.

3 Choose one set of rhyming words. Try and make your own two lines that rhyme.

CHALLENGE YOURSELF

How much do you waste every day? Take this waste challenge for the next week.

Make a waste diary (ask your teacher for a blank diary to fill in). Every day, for one week, write down each item you throw away.

Keep your waste diary for an activity later in this unit.

Reading

Recycling

1 Read these two posters with a friend. Discuss the posters and the opinions given in each poster. Then answer the questions.

Why is your recycling programme failing?

1 People don't care!

2 People don't understand why recycling is necessary.

3 If there are no separate bins, people won't separate waste.

4 If bins aren't properly labelled, people get confused.

 2 Discuss these questions in your group. Use the words in the box to help you.

a Which poster has the best message? Say why you think so.

b Do you agree with what the writer says in the first poster? Say why or why not.

c What do you think of the second poster?

d Do you agree with any of the points in the second poster? Explain why to your group.

positive	negative	hopeful	hopeless	helpful	unhelpful

Design your own poster about recycling waste.

- Think of the message you would like to share.
- Use big bold writing for your main message.
- Decorate your poster with artwork.
- Display your posters in school.

Vocabulary

Match the word in column A to its meaning in column B. Write each word with its meaning in your notebook.

A	B
rubbish	using something again for the same purpose or for a different purpose
recycling	damaging a natural **environment** by throwing waste matter in it
packaging	unwanted or used things that are thrown away
polluting	the plastic and paper that things are wrapped in

Spelling

1 First say these words out loud. Then learn to spell them.

reduce	reuse	recycle	package	plastic

2 Work in pairs. Use the words in the box to complete these sentences.
  a If we _____ the amount of plastic we use, the amount of waste we make will be less.
  b I am going to _____ this glass bottle and plant something in it.
  c If there is a choice, I will always avoid buying _____ bottles.
  d Do we need to _____ fruit like bananas and oranges?
  e My mum says we need to _____ all our plastic bottles.

Try this

Read this poem about waste. Then act out the poem with a partner, with one of you playing the grandmother and one the young boy. Present the poem to the rest of the class.

My gran says,

You will pay!

We didn't used,

To live this way.

Wash it out,

Put it away,

Use again,

Another day.

I say,

Use it today,

No one cares,

Throw it away.

Buy again,

Another day!

Speaking and listening

How to recycle waste

LET'S TALK

Does your family recycle its waste? Discuss this in small groups. Use these questions to help you.

- Does your community have a recycling programme?
- How does this programme work?
- Do you separate different kinds of waste at home?

- What kind of waste gets stored in different containers?
- Why is this **important**?
- What more do you think can be done to recycle waste in your community?

CHALLENGE YOURSELF

1   Work with a partner. Look at these two photographs. Decide on a caption for each photograph.

▲ Photo A   ▲ Photo B

2   Match these words to the correct bin in Photo A:
- General waste
- Hazardous waste
- Recyclable waste.

3   What do you think the green bin is for?

4   Look at the items in the box below. Into which bin would you put these things?

a broken cup	a cardboard box	a used battery
a plastic bottle	grass cuttings	

5   Now write three sentences, explaining how you think the waste from photo A ended up in photo B.

6   Discuss your sentences in class.
   a   How many people have similar sentences?
   b   Do you think all the waste from the bins in the picture went to the same place?
   c   Talk about the different places each type of waste might have gone.

Listen to Audio 3.2, which is a dialogue between a talk show host and the head of a recycling programme called *CycleApp!* Your teacher will play the recording twice.

1 Here is a list of sentences. Some of them are true, and some are not. As you listen, write down the letters of the sentences that are true.
   a The guest's name is Anne Brown.
   b Her company is called *CycleApp!*
   c They collect waste from over 4000 households.
   d All you have to do is send a message, and they come and collect your waste.
   e They charge people extra for re-sorting their waste.
   f They have three small trucks.
   g The garden waste gets made into compost.
   h Most of the waste goes to the landfill.

 2 Discuss the sentences with your partner.
   ● How many of the sentences are true?
   ● Do you have the same lists? Work together to produce one final, true, list.

Try this

Not all plastic can be recycled. A lot of the plastic people put into recycling containers ends up going to a landfill, because it cannot be recycled.

CHALLENGE YOURSELF

How are you doing on your weekly waste chart from the first lesson? Discuss your lists in a group:
● Who has the most waste so far?
● Who has the least waste?
● Which waste items does everyone have?
● How do you think you can reduce the amount of waste you produce?
● What is the most unusual waste item in the group?

Collect plastic waste from home for a week. Wash each item before you handle it. Bring a selection of your plastic items to class, for an activity later in the week.

Use of English

Conditional clauses with 'if'

Do you remember?

The table below shows first conditional clauses with 'if'.

If clause	Main clause
If + simple present	Future (will)
If this thing happens	Then this is very likely to happen

We use the first conditional when we want to talk about actions in the future which are very likely to happen. For example: If you send me an email, I will reply immediately.

The table below shows zero conditional clauses with 'if'.

If clause	Main clause
If + simple present	Simple present
If this thing happens	Then this thing happens too

We use the zero conditional when we want to say things we know are true. We often use the zero conditional to talk about science facts.

Try this

 Read this short extract about landfill sites with your partner. Take turns reading it to each other.

Landfill sites

A landfill site is a place where people dump waste. All sorts of rubbish ends up in landfill sites: household waste, leftovers from restaurants, broken furniture and waste from building and **industry**.

In the old days, people used to just dump rubbish in piles on top of the ground. This could be very smelly, and often liquid waste would soak into the ground and pollute natural waters and streams.

A good landfill site nowadays is dug out of the ground and lined with plastic, so no toxic waste can sink into the ground water. They are usually found outside towns, so the waste is kept away from people.

If we want to keep waste out of landfills, we have to reduce the waste we make. We can recycle more easily, if governments make recycling a part of normal waste collection. If everyone has a recycling bin, this will help to reduce the problem.

PRACTISE

How many of your own 'zero conditional' and 'first conditional' sentences can you make up? Work with a partner. The 'Do you remember?' box on page 44 will help you. Write at least five of your own sentences for zero conditional and five for first conditional.

PRACTISE

1   Match the clauses from column A to those in column B.

A	B
If we recycle more,	I will be very annoyed!
The school needs to have a recycling bin	I will miss taking out the garbage.
If all the governments in the world ban plastic packaging,	so that we can recycle at school.
If my sister drops her **sweet** wrappers on the floor again,	I will take it all out and sort it into the correct bins.
It will be quite fun	we will reduce the amount of waste that goes into landfill.
If I wake up late	if we make art from recycled materials.
If I find the rubbish unsorted,	it will help clean up the earth very much.

2   Complete these sentences in your notebook.
a   If you throw rubbish in a rubbish bin, _____.
b   If you don't want something old and broken, _____.
c   If toxic waste leaks out of a landfill _____.
d   If you line a landfill with plastic _____.

Present continuous

The present continuous (or progressive) tense describes an action that continues to happen in the present. It uses this form:

am/is/are + _____ing

(form of the verb 'to be' + present participle)

I am using the app.	You are listening.
They are recycling.	She/he is collecting waste.
We are helping.	It is becoming popular.

PRACTISE

Complete these sentences by choosing the correct form of the verb in brackets.

1   The company (is/are) recycling waste.
2   Her uncle (is/are) developing an app.
3   We (is/are) recycling our old clothes.
4   They (is/are) making art to sell to tourists.
5   He (is/are) visiting a recycling company.

PRACTISE

Now change the verb in brackets into the present continuous tense.
1   We (to recycle) our waste at home.
2   My family (to use) different bins for different waste.
3   You (to go) to Dubai to visit.
4   I (to help) with the waste project.
5   They (to make) art out of waste glass.

Speaking and listening

Dumping waste

China says NO!

Until recently, countries like the USA and the UK sent all their excess rubbish to China, where it was recycled. But in 2018, China stopped accepting the rubbish. The Chinese government does not want the West's polluting waste any longer. If other countries say no, what will the western countries do with their waste?

 1 Discuss the short newspaper article in your group. Choose a scribe for your group.
- Talk about the question in the article: 'If other countries say no, what will the western countries do with their waste?'
- Decide on the best answer for your group.
- The scribe should write your group's answer on the board.
- How many groups have the same answer?
- Which is the best answer, in your opinion?

 2 Listen to Audio 3.3, which is a short article on how western countries have been dumping their excess waste in China, and what happened when China finally said 'no!'
- Listen carefully for the facts.
- Make short notes as you listen. Your teacher will play the audio three times.
- Compare your notes with a partner. Help each other to fill in anything that is missing.
- You will need your notes for the next exercise, which is a debate about the rights and wrongs of exporting waste to other countries.

> **CHALLENGE YOURSELF**
>
> Elect two teams to debate this question:
>
> 'Should each country be responsible for their own waste, or should countries be allowed to sell their waste to anyone who is a willing buyer?'
>
> One side argues for selling waste (they are the **proposition**). The other side argues against this (they are the **opposition**); they want countries to sort out their own rubbish problems.

Do you remember?

Debating

1 2 3

One side argues for the issue.
They are the **proposition**.

The chair introduces
the debate, keeps
order and counts
the vote.

1 2 3

The other side argues against the issue.
They are the **opposition.**

LET'S TALK

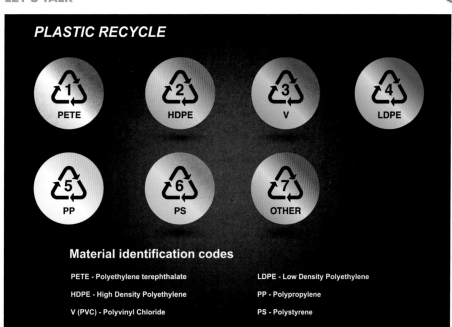

PLASTIC RECYCLE

PETE

HDPE

V

LDPE

PP

PS

OTHER

Material identification codes

PETE - Polyethylene terephthalate

HDPE - High Density Polyethylene

V (PVC) - Polyvinyl Chloride

LDPE - Low Density Polyethylene

PP - Polypropylene

PS - Polystyrene

Remember your waste plastic?

1 Work in your group to divide the plastic according to the labels on each
   item, saying whether the item is recyclable or not. Use the material
   identification codes above to help you.
2 Prepare a short talk about your findings. Explain to the class which plastics
   can be recycled.
3 Discuss your ideas for reusing the plastic containers that cannot be recycled.

Your teacher will select a scribe to write down the class's ideas for reusing
plastic containers on the board.

Use of English

Vocabulary

▲ You should never waste food

PRACTISE

Choose the correct word in brackets to complete these sentences.

1 The (main/mane) reason for recycling is to reduce the massive amount of (waste/waist) humans produce.

2 Some metals like (steal/steel) can be recycled; others like (led/lead) cannot.

3 Food should never be (waisted/wasted)!

4 Many recycling companies make big (prophets/profits).

5 My mum says not wasting food gives her (piece/peace) of mind.

Spelling

Try this

You can make many words with the root word 'cycle'.

1 See how many new words you and your friend can make from the part-words in the box.

2 Once you have made a list of new words, try and use each one in a sentence.

tri-		-ing
bi-	cycle	-ed
re-		-able

1 Read this article from the internet about recycling bottles.

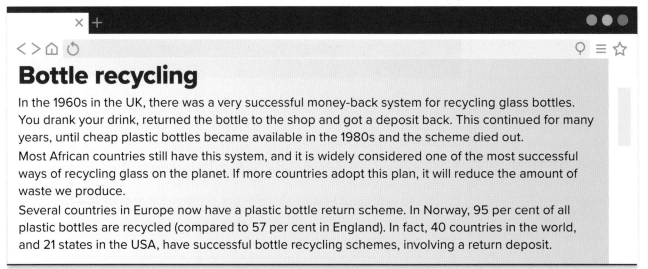

Bottle recycling

In the 1960s in the UK, there was a very successful money-back system for recycling glass bottles. You drank your drink, returned the bottle to the shop and got a deposit back. This continued for many years, until cheap plastic bottles became available in the 1980s and the scheme died out.

Most African countries still have this system, and it is widely considered one of the most successful ways of recycling glass on the planet. If more countries adopt this plan, it will reduce the amount of waste we produce.

Several countries in Europe now have a plastic bottle return scheme. In Norway, 95 per cent of all plastic bottles are recycled (compared to 57 per cent in England). In fact, 40 countries in the world, and 21 states in the USA, have successful bottle recycling schemes, involving a return deposit.

PRACTISE
Answer these questions in your notebook, using the information from the reading text about recycling bottles.

1 If you return your bottle, you will
_____.

2 If we recycle glass, we will
_____.

3 If the UK starts this system
_____.

4 If you do not recycle your bottle, you will not
_____.

5 If people cut plastic waste, we will not
_____.

DID YOU KNOW?

If an adverb has more than two syllables, you add 'more' or 'most'.

DID YOU KNOW?

Adverbial phrases tell you more about a verb, just like adverbs do. They do not have a verb.

Adverbial phrases of manner tell you *how,* for example:

He ran as quickly as the wind.

 2 Talk about the article in your group. What other ideas do you have for reducing waste?

Start like this:
● If we reuse more …
● If we recycle more of our waste …
● If we reduce …

We use the first conditional if there is a very real possibility that something will happen in the future.

If + condition + result

If + will/will not + present simple

For example:

If he studies hard, he will pass his exam.

Adverbs

Adverbs tell you more about verbs. You can use adverbs to compare actions. Here are some examples.

Adverb	Comparative	Superlative
fast	faster	fastest
high	higher	highest
easy	easier	easiest
quickly	more quickly	most quickly
carefully	more carefully	most carefully
badly	worse	the worst
well	better	the best
much	more	the most
little	less	the least

PRACTISE

Complete these sentences by using the correct form of the adverb in brackets.

1 China has done (much/more/the most) in terms of plastic recycling.

2 My brother does (less/little/the least) than anyone in our family about recycling.

3 People in my country are (well/better/the best) at recycling, because for them everything has a use.

4 We need to move (quickly/more quickly/most quickly) if we are to have any hope of saving our oceans.

5 Plastic waste is (badly/worse/the worst) than other kinds of waste.

6 The figures are (high/higher/highest) every day.

Reading

Tackling food waste

1 Read this article, adapted from the *Arab News* **website**, written by Asheel Bashraheel, on 21 January 2020.

A Saudi food waste startup company is helping to feed animals

Carbon CPU is a **biotechnology startup** company specialising in turning food waste into fatty acids for use as livestock **nutrients**.

What this means to people like us is that this group of young **entrepreneurs** has found a way to turn our waste food into nutritious food for animals.

Launched through the post-graduate startup accelerator program (TAQADAM) of King Abdullah University of Science and Technology (KAUST), the venture was co-founded by Bin Bian, Jiajie Xu, Yara Aldrees, Sara Al-Eid and Professor Pascal Saikaly.

The idea behind the **enterprise** began to take shape in 2018.

Similar to most countries, Saudi Arabia has a food waste problem, but Carbon CPU thought of using waste in a way that caused less harm to the environment and also benefited the animal feed industry.

'Over 90 per cent of food waste in Saudi Arabia is dumped into landfills,' said Aldrees. 'This produces a lot of gas, and contributes to global warming and air **pollution**.' Water and soil were also being contaminated, she added. 'We're trying to solve those issues, too.'

The team found that animal farms often struggled to provide enough food nutrients for livestock such as cows and sheep.

Carbon CPU's **technology** uses a specially developed, **eco-friendly** reactor to help convert food waste into fatty acids, which are then added to animal feed, to make it more nutritious.

The startup initially faced many challenges that KAUST helped to resolve. As individuals coming from backgrounds mainly in engineering and science, the team lacked the know-how in business that its project needed.

'KAUST made up for our lack of business thinking through training on how to solve business issues and create business modules and find the right customers for our product,' said Bian.

Source: www.arabnews.com

2 Discuss these questions about the article with your partner.
   a Who is the writer of the article?
   b What does the writer think of the start-up company?
   c What does the company do?
   d How do you think the people in the photograph feel?
   e Where was the photograph taken, do you think?

Try this

Look up these words in your dictionary. Copy the words into your notebook. Write their meaning next to them.
- Startup
- Entrepreneur
- Biotechnology
- Nutritious
- Accelerator

PRACTISE

Answer these questions about the article in your notebook.
1 What does the company Carbon CPU do?
2 How many co-founders does this company have?
3 How much food waste is dumped into landfills in Saudi Arabia?
4 Why is this a bad thing for the environment?
5 What two natural resources are also being contaminated?
6 What problem is the team solving for farmers?
7 What does Carbon CPU's reactor do?
8 What does the word 'eco-friendly' mean?
9 Who helped the team with their problems?
10 Who, or what, is KAUST?

CHALLENGE YOURSELF

Think about what you have learned in this unit. How do other companies get rid of waste? Write down what you remember.

Writing

Write a blog

 1 Look at these posters about zero food waste. Talk about them with your group.

    a What do the posters have in common?

    b What is different about each poster?

    c Which of the posters do you like best? Can you say why?

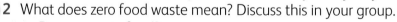 **2** What does zero food waste mean? Discuss this in your group.

    a Do you waste food?

    b How can you prevent food waste?

    c What can you do with leftover food?

Make your own poster about zero food waste.
- Your poster should have one main idea.
- Make the writing bold and easy to read.
- Decorate your poster with drawings about zero food waste.

CHALLENGE YOURSELF

You are going to write a blog giving **zero-waste** tips for teens. Prepare like this:
- Start by sharing ideas in your group.
- Use the posters to give you extra ideas.
- Make short notes of your top five zero-waste ideas.

If you have internet access, search online for 'how to start a blog for free' – you should get a page which looks like the one below.

Write out your five top zero-waste tips. You should have some good ideas from the group discussion and making your poster.

Swap with a friend. Read each other's writing and correct any mistakes you find.

Finally, when you are happy with your text, follow the instructions for starting your own blog.

How to start a blog for free

1 Pick a blog name. Emphasise what your blog posts will be about with a creative name.
2 Choose your blog template. Customise the design of your blog to match your style.
3 Start writing posts.
4 Connect your domain.
5 Publish posts and go live.
6 Share your posts.

Self check

Take out your waste diary from lesson 1.
- How many waste items did you throw away each day?
- What is your waste total for the week?
- What can you do to reduce your waste? Write down three ideas.

What can you do?

Read and review what you can do.
- I can talk, read and write about waste and recycling.
- I can use the present continuous tense and adverbs to describe recycling.
- I can discuss newspaper articles and posters and give my own opinion.
- I can listen to arguments and the opinions of others.
- I can have a debate about whose responsibility it is to get rid of waste.
- I can write a waste diary for a week and a blog about zero food waste.
- I can use 'if' clauses in zero and first conditional to discuss what will happen if we do not reduce, reuse and recycle.

Now you have completed Unit 3, you may like to try the Unit 3 online knowledge test if you are using the Boost eBook.

Review Units 1–3

PRACTISE

Read and complete the sentences. Choose the best words from the box for each sentence.

decorations	recycle	startup	landfill	special
eco-friendly	funny	fireworks	celebrations	alone

1 My friends are all very _____ to me!

2 Did you read that _____ story on Facebook yesterday? I had a good laugh!

3 She likes to be _____ sometimes so that she can read a book.

4 When do the new year _____ take place in Malaysia this year?

5 Many countries set off _____ to celebrate the new year.

6 Do you put up any _____ in your home for this celebration?

7 Solar power is an _____ way of generating power.

8 You can _____ plastic, glass and paper. Don't waste it!

9 A _____ site is the place where people dump waste.

10 This _____ company is very new and it aims to reuse waste.

Try this

What does the underlined expression in each sentence mean? Choose the best answer.

1 We have a lot in common.
   a things that are similar or similar **interests**
   b things that are not special or unusual

2 I like to chat to a person face-to-face, not online.
   a looking at someone who is opposite or near you
   b talking to someone on the internet

3 We were covered in coloured dye after the Holi festival.
   a to have something all over yourself
   b to have clothes of many colours

4 Mara and Malik started the count down to the new year at 20 seconds before midnight.
   a to count numbers backwards until a specific time
   b to count numbers aloud

5 It is as easy as pie to separate your rubbish before you throw it away.
   a delicious
   b very simple

Work in pairs.
Complete these
sentences in two
different ways.
Choose your best
ideas and read them
to the class.

1 We bought
   candles so that
   we …
2 The people are
   wearing costumes
   because …
3 The river
   is polluted
   because …
4 Friends can help
   you with many
   things such as …
5 There is too much
   waste, therefore …

PRACTISE

Choose the correct words to complete each sentence.

1 We often (go/goes) to watch the baseball match at the weekend.
2 Hi Darren. Could (you/your) please show (mine/me) where the library is?
3 The show (was enjoy/was enjoyed) by everyone.
4 What is that place famous (of/for)?
5 The street (was/were) full of people in colourful costumes.
6 When were the celebrations (holded/held)? In May or June?
7 Paula and I went out in the street (so that/although) we could watch the celebrations.
8 My family (to use/uses) different bins for different waste.
9 Plastic waste is (badly/worse/the worst) than other kinds of waste.
10 If governments ban all plastic packaging, we (will be able/are able) to reduce waste.

PRACTISE

Rewrite this paragraph in your notebook with the correct punctuation.

> I live in dubai in an apartment on the fifth floor we use an app called homecycle you use the app when you want the recycling people to come and collect your waste it is becoming very popular in the city it saves you taking your waste out in the heat says my father i agree

Try this

Choose one of the photographs below. Write a description of the photograph.

The description should be one paragraph of four to five sentences.

CHALLENGE

Write a short blog that explains how you feel about recycling waste. Write about 100 words and try to make this interesting for your readers.

4 Travelling by train

In this unit you will:
- listen to a short talk about travelling by train
- listen to a conversation at a railway station
- talk about different types of train travel and experiences
- read non-fiction accounts about **bullet** trains and metros
- read an extract from a story which involves a trip on a train
- use prepositions in phrases with nouns and adjectives
- use past continuous and present perfect forms to describe events
- write a description of people and places on a train **journey**.

Speaking and listening

Describing trains

Do you travel by train? Have you ever travelled on a train similar to one of those in the photographs?

Now work in pairs. Match these descriptions to the photographs on page 56.

This is a **cargo** train that transports goods or freight in containers.

This train has sleeper **carriages**. Passengers can book a bed in one of these carriages and sleep while they travel.

This train is travelling across a special bridge which was built for trains.

This train station is crowded with people getting off trains or going to catch their trains.

Older trains burn coal in order to move. **Steam** or smoke comes out of the chimneys of these trains. They are often called steam trains.

This train travels at more than 300 km per hour. It is often called a bullet train.

Try this

Now add one sentence of your own to describe each photograph. For example:

You can buy food and train tickets at the train station.

Modern electric trains are faster and cleaner than steam trains.

 Listen carefully to the conversation in Audio 4.1 and then write your answers to these questions in your notebook.
1 What are the names of the two girls?
2 Where are they?
3 Why is the second speaker not taking a plane to visit her cousins?
4 What time does the second speaker's train leave the station?
5 How long is the journey?
6 What do these words and phrases from the conversation mean?
   a A trip
   b I'm off to my cousin's
   c Eco-friendly
   d To have a fear

HINT
Train times are usually very precise. For example, a train may leave at 9:38 (say: nine thirty-eight) or 21:42 (say: twenty-one forty-two).

PRACTISE
 Work in groups of four. Role-play a short scene in which you meet at a train station. Ask each other questions about where you are going and what time your train is leaving.

57

Speaking and listening

Listen to a podcast

🎧 Listen to Marco in Audio 4.2, who blogs about his travels on trains. He is **reflecting** on why train journeys inspire him to write.

Try this

💬 Now work in pairs. Listen to the podcast again and work out the meanings of these words from the context of the blog:

- Crowded
- Bumped
- To put up with
- There is something about trains ...

Share your ideas with the rest of the class.

DID YOU KNOW?

Trains and metro trains run according to timetables. You can use apps to find the timetables or you can download these timetables on your phone from the internet. You can also look at the electronic departure and arrival boards in the stations. You can sometimes also get printed maps and timetables of the schedules.

LET'S TALK

Work in pairs. Download a timetable for the place where you live or use the train notice boards below. Ask and answer questions about the timetable. For example:

- Can you tell me about trains to ...?
- At what time can I get a train to ...?
- From which **platform** does the train to ... leave?
- If I miss this train, is there another train I can catch?
- How do I get to ...?
- Is the train on time?
- Have you ever been to ...? Is it far?

Departures		Plat	Expt
15:41	Gloucester	9	On time
	Via Bristol Parkway		
15:44	Westbury	7	On time
15:44	Exeter St David's	6	On time
15:45	Bristol Parkway		Cancelled
15:51	London Waterloo	12	On time
15:53	Taunton	8	On time
15:54	Cardiff Central	9	On time
Page 1 of 2			15:43:42

Departures		Plat	Expt
16:00	via Birmingham New St		
16:00	London Paddington	15	On time
16:03	Avonmouth	5	On time
16:15	Bristol Parkway	7	On time
16:18	Weston-super-Mare	15	On time
16:22	via Southampton Ctl		
16:24	Cardiff Central	3	On time
16:26	Weston-super-Mare	10	On time
Page 2 of 2			15:43:42

Try this

Listen to the train station schedule announcement in Audio 4.3 and complete these sentences. Use words and times from the box.

7:04	station	6:22	6:47	6:24	6	time	two

Welcome to Waterloo _____. All trains are currently running on _____.

The _____ train to Basingstoke leaves in _____ minutes from platform _____. This is a fast train which does not stop at all stations. The next train leaves at _____.

The suburban service train to Alton, stopping at Woking, leaves at _____. The next train leaves at _____.

Use of English

Phrases to describe journeys

Do you remember?

A phrase is a group of two or more words, without a verb. For example:

at the station
on your phone
at 6:15 from platform 7

Sometimes we use prepositions before adjectives and nouns in prepositional phrases.

Prepositional phrases start with prepositions.

Some prepositional phrases describe and tell us more about a noun in the main part of the sentence.

For example:

She will be a <u>passenger</u> on the fast train to Basingstoke.

She is on <u>holiday</u> with her older cousins.

PRACTISE

Copy these sentences into your notebook and underline the prepositional phrases.

1 This is a suburban train to Alton.

2 We sat in a carriage with many passengers.

3 What is in that suitcase under the seat?

4 She has a fear of steam trains.

5 I can see some sheep beside the train.

6 The book with the tattered old cover is my favourite travel story!

Try this

 Work in pairs. Choose the correct preposition to complete each sentence. Share your sentences with your group or with the class.

1 She wrote a story _____ a train journey.
   a about
   b by
   c of
   d over

2 We have often taken the fast train _____ Birmingham.
   a for
   b to
   c by
   d under

3 Saira went on a holiday _____ her school class.
   a of
   b near
   c with
   d for

4 The suitcases _____ the platform belong to the passengers sitting in the waiting room.
   a on
   b in
   c for
   d by

Describing events

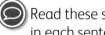 Read these sentences aloud with a partner. Can you identify the verb tense in each sentence?

- The writer Paul Theroux has often written about his train journeys.
- I have never taken a train to school.

Do you remember?

We use the present perfect tense to describe an action that we did in the past and that we are still doing or hope to do in the future.

We use the verb 'have/has' with the past participle to form this verb tense.

CHALLENGE YOURSELF

Write a paragraph of six to eight sentences about the kinds of places you would like to visit on holiday. Your holiday must include train travel. Use the present perfect tense in at least four of your sentences. You might like to look at the photographs to give you some ideas.

PRACTISE

Choose the correct form of the verb in each sentence. Write the complete correct sentence in your notebook.

1 She (has always enjoyed/have always enjoyed) reading novels about travelling.

2 The girls (are often taking/have often taken) the train from Waterloo station to Woking.

3 I (haven't been/hasn't be) there for many years.

4 (Has/Have) you ever (took/taken) the train to Mumbai?

5 I have never (to see/seen) such a crowded railway station!

6 Meera (has been/have be) on holiday with her family in Singapore for three days.

Reading

Railway blogs

As you saw earlier in this unit, Marco blogs about train journeys. In these two extracts from his blog he tells us more about the Métro trains in Paris and about the bullet trains in Japan.

www.marcostrains.com

Marco – on the trains

Tōkaidō Shinkansen in Japan

I have been lucky enough to visit Japan twice and travel on the famous bullet trains. A bullet train is a train that travels, well, very fast – as fast as a bullet. It has the shape of a bullet too. The official name is a 'high-speed train'. The newer bullet trains can travel more than 250 km per hour. Compare that with driving in a car at an average speed of 100 km an hour!

▲ Trains on the Tōkaidō Shinkansen high-speed railway system in Japan

High-speed trains have operated in Japan since 1964, when the Tōkaidō Shinkansen was opened. The train system connects all the major cities in Japan and is the best way to get around the country.

Since then, many other countries such as France, China, the United Kingdom, Germany, Italy, Russia, South Korea and Turkey have built high-speed rail systems. In Europe you can travel from one country to another on a high-speed train.

The Métro in Paris, France

Paris is one of my favourite cities and again I have been lucky enough to go there several times. On my visits I have always used the **underground** railway system (called Le Métro) to get around. It is one of the busiest transport systems in the world, but it is simple and easy to use. Last year while I was visiting, I made at least six trips on the Métro every day.

The Métro has operated since 1900. The word 'metro' is an abbreviation of the word 'metropolitan' which means a city area (the French word is 'métropolitain'). Most of the trains run **underground**. Each Métro line has a different colour and number, so it is easy to find on a map. There is one problem though. If you use a wheelchair, it can be difficult to get around as many stations only have stairs and no lifts to get up from and down to the trains.

I have often taken the lines that stop in Châtelet–Les Halles, as it is easy to find connecting trains and metros there. Last year, while I was travelling on the Métro, I met another blogger who also likes to write about trains. We were both blogging while sitting on the train.

Next year I hope to visit Moscow and travel on the metro there. People say the stations are beautiful!

Vocabulary and spelling

PRACTISE

1 Work in pairs. Find synonyms in the reading text for the underlined words in each sentence.
   a Have you ever travelled on the <u>high-speed</u> trains in Japan?
   b The railway system connects all the <u>big and important</u> cities to each other.
   c The <u>underground train system</u> in Paris is easy to use.
   d They made a <u>trip</u> to India last month.

2 Explain what these words mean in your own words.
   a A bullet train
   b Metropolitan
   c A lift
   d A blogger

3 Choose the best meaning for the underlined words in these sentences.
   a 'Paris is one of <u>my favourite</u> cities,' said Marco.
      – Marco likes visiting Paris.
      – Marco does not like Paris very much.
   b It can be difficult <u>to get around.</u>
      – to find a round place
      – to travel from one place to another
   c It is not easy to find <u>connecting trains.</u>
      – trains that are joined together
      – trains that stop at the same station so that you can get off one train and take another train
   d The Métro <u>has operated</u> since 1900.
      – The Métro started to work in 1900 and still works now.
      – The Métro stopped working in 1900 and no longer works.

Try this

Work out what words these jumbled-up letters make and write them correctly. Check your answers with your partner. Then practise writing these words. Break the longer words up into syllables to make this easier.
- neyjour
- veltra
- nectcon
- niart
- groundunder
- noistat

CHALLENGE YOURSELF

Work in groups of five or six students. Imagine that you are at a train station or an underground station, looking around. Take turns to say what you can see. Repeat what you hear and add your own words. For example:

I can see a bullet train!

I can see a bullet train and the departure boards.

I can see a bullet train, the departure boards and lots of suitcases.

HINT
Look at the photographs in this unit for ideas!

Use of English

Continuous tenses

Continuous tense verbs are useful in storytelling and reports because they can describe events and actions that are happening now, will happen in the future or were happening at a certain time in the past.

Do you remember?

Do you remember how to form verbs in the present continuous tense?

Look at these examples with a partner. Identify the verbs in the present continuous tense and explain to your partner how each verb is formed.

- I am travelling by train to Scotland.
- They are watching the passengers get on the train.

We can also use verbs in the past continuous tense. For example:

> Last year, while I was visiting Paris, I made at least six trips on the Metro every day.

To form the past continuous tense, we use the '-ing' form (the present participle) of the verb with the past tense form of the verb 'to be'.

PRACTISE

Work in pairs. Find the verbs in the following sentences and identify the sentences in which the past continuous tense is used. Read the past continuous tense verbs aloud.

1 Last year, while I was travelling on the Paris Métro, I met another blogger who also likes to write about trains. We were both working on our blogs while sitting on the train. I was writing a blog on my tablet and she was dictating a blog on her phone.

2 My sister and I were waiting at the train station when the accident happened. The platform was crowded. A child was running along the platform when he tripped over one of the many suitcases. Fortunately, the boy only had a few bruises and he did not fall onto the railway line!

3 Joe and I went from Naples to Rome by train last year. As we were leaving Naples, we saw Mount Vesuvius, which is a volcano. The last time it erupted was in 1944. But as we were racing along on the train, I thought I saw smoke ...!

We use the past continuous tense to describe an event that took place in the past, while another event was taking place. Look at these examples. Can you see that there are two clauses in each sentence? The verb in one clause is in the simple past tense and the other verb is in the past continuous tense.

As I was getting onto the train, someone pushed in front of me.

I was travelling on the train, when I met Mr Newby.

PRACTISE

Rewrite this paragraph, using the past continuous forms of the verbs in brackets.

> As we got on the train, people (to push) their way into the compartments. My sister sat down but I (to stand) in the corridor when the train started moving again. I **bumped** into other people. As I tried to get to my seat, other people (to unpack) their bedrolls and baskets of food. There wasn't very much room to move!

Try this

Work with a partner. Think about something that you were doing earlier in the day or in the past. Then think of something that happened while you were doing this. Make sentences to describe these events. Start like this:

This morning/Last week/Yesterday, while I was _____, _____.

Make three sentences each. Do this orally, then write your sentences out correctly. Check your spelling. Make sure one verb in each sentence is in the past continuous tense and the other verb is in the simple past tense.

CHALLENGE YOURSELF

Describe what you see in the photograph and what you think happened. Use at least two verbs in the past continuous tense. You should write five to six sentences in your notebook.

Reading

Read a story

Before you read, predict what you think this story is about.

The Train to Aunty's

Amina was playing a game on her tablet, when a bird flew down and startled her. Neeria, her ten-year-old sister, who was sitting next to her, smiled and flicked one of her long **plaits** over her shoulder as the bird flew off once more.

There were a number of people on the station. Some were waiting **patiently** while others were chatting to their friends or texting on their phones. Amina hoped that the train would not be late. Then she jiggled one leg **impatiently** and continued with her game.

A siren heralded the arrival of a train, which rattled in at the platform across from where Amina and Neeria were sitting. People were soon racing with their luggage trolleys and suitcases towards the train. They pushed in among the crowd of passengers, some of whom were **disembarking** and others who were trying to board the train.

'Let's go,' said Neeria.

'This isn't our train,' muttered Amina. 'Our train is late. It should have been here 10 minutes ago. I hate this.'

'Oh well, I'm hungry,' said Neeria, and she took out her lunchbox. The train pulled away from the platform and calm descended once more on the station.

But soon the tracks in front of Amina were vibrating again and the air was suddenly alive with noise and activity as the siren sounded once more.

'That's us!' shouted Amina, grabbing Neeria's hand. Amina and Neeria collected their bags and packages. Amina held tightly to her little sister's hand as the train screeched to a stop in front of them.

'Why are we going to Aunty's house?' asked Neeria happily as they were settling down.

'Because … Oh I don't know,' said Amina. 'I think Aunty has been sick and she needs some help.'

'Are all these people also going to Aunty's house?' asked Neeria, looking around at the other passengers.

'NO! Of course not … I don't know,' said Amina.

'Why are they …?' Neeria stopped. 'Oh, I suppose you don't know that either, do you? Well, never mind. I'll make up my own stories about them …'

Vocabulary and spelling

Try this

Work in pairs. Read these sentences and discuss what they mean. Choose the best meaning for the underlined words in the sentences.

1   The train <u>screeched</u> to a stop in front of them.
    a   made a loud noise   b   shouted

2   Neeria <u>flicked</u> one of her long plaits over her shoulder.
    a   to comb   b   make something move with your fingers

3   <u>Calm descended once more</u> on the station.
    a   became quiet again   b   people came down

4   She <u>jiggled</u> one leg impatiently.
    a   moved   b   scratched

5   A siren <u>heralded</u> the arrival of a train.
    a   announced   b   sang

Write your answers to these questions in your notebook.

6   Where are Amina and Neeria when the story begins?
7   Where are they going?
8   Write down two things that the people at the train station were doing.
9   Do you think Neeria was happy to go to Aunty's?
10 Why did Amina grab her sister's hand before they got on the train?
11 Do you think all the people on the train are going to Aunty's house?
12 What do you think Neeria will do while she is on the train?

PRACTISE

Listen to Audio 4.4. These sentences are in the past continuous tense. After you have listened, practise reading them aloud with a partner and identify the present participle verbs in the sentences.

1   Some people were waiting patiently and others were chatting to their friends or texting on their phones.
2   But soon the tracks in front of Amina were vibrating again.
3   People were racing with their luggage trolleys and suitcases towards the train.

HINT
Which participles have double consonants?

Try this

Learn to spell these participles. What do you notice about the spelling? Write each word in the present simple form first and compare the forms with the participles.

travelling	running	playing
sitting	waiting	listening
chatting	watching	

Speaking and listening

Describe what you see

LET'S TALK

Work in groups. Think about what you can see from a train window. Look at the photographs here, which were taken from train windows. Describe what you see. Make at least two sentences to describe each picture.

Try this

Listen to Audio 4.5, which features part of a poem called 'From a Railway Carriage'. It is a very well-known poem by a Scottish poet called Robert Louis Stevenson. As you listen, try to hear the rhythm (movement) of the train in the words.

1   Talk about what the poet saw from the train window. Which of the following does he mention? Do you know what all the words mean?

bridges	horses	ditches	patients	snow
cattle	houses	pylons	rain	stations
hills	meadows	turbines	sheep	

2   Now think about the speed of the train in the poem. What do you think this expression in the poem means?

in the wink of an eye

PRACTISE

Work in pairs and read some of the lines of this poem inspired by the poem you have just listened to. Then read it faster a second time. It is almost like a tongue twister but if you read it correctly you will feel as if you are sitting in a moving train!

'On a Fast Train'

(Inspired by RL Stevenson)

Faster than buses, faster than horses

Past bridges and ditches, houses and hedges.

We **race** at 300 kilometres an hour.

Round the fields and the farms and the towns and the tower

Past mountains and pylons, through day after night

Through sunshine and shadow and colour and light.

And then, in a wink of an eye, it's all clear

The journey is over and the station is here!

CHALLENGE YOURSELF

In pairs, make up two or four lines of a poem about sitting in a train. You do not have to write full sentences.

You could also try to write like RL Stevenson. Use the same rhythm as he does. This means you need to choose words to make the same number of syllables in each line.

You could start like this:

Faster than _____, faster than _____

_____ and _____ and _____ and _____

Remember to use plural nouns.

Writing

Write an account of a train journey

Many authors have written about train journeys, and you can too. Here are a few ideas to get you started.

Do you remember?

It is a good idea to use connectives to link words, clauses, sentences and ideas when we speak and when we write. This makes our writing and speaking more interesting.

Connectives can be words such as 'and', 'because', 'or', 'but' or 'although'. They can also be words that help to describe a sequence of events such as 'then', 'after that', 'before' and 'after'. Words such as 'when' and 'while' can also connect ideas.

Pronouns can also help to connect ideas because they refer back to nouns.

PRACTISE

Read this paragraph again and identify all the connectives.

> There were a number of people on the station. Some were waiting patiently while others were chatting to their friends or texting on their phones. Amina hoped that the train would not be late. Then she jiggled one leg impatiently and continued with her game.

Try this

Work in pairs. Read the sentences and try to connect them into logical paragraphs. Do this orally and try out different connectives until you are satisfied. Then write the paragraphs and share them with the class.

1 We got on the train in Naples. We found our seats. The train went very fast. We saw Mount Vesuvius. We arrived in Rome. It was late at night.
2 Luc and Lee got on the train. Lee held on to her brother's hand. She had not been on a train before. She was excited. She was afraid. The train came. Luc helped Lee onto the train.

CHALLENGE YOURSELF
Find a photograph on the internet or in a magazine showing people travelling on a train or waiting at a train station. Write a description of the photograph. You could also try to imagine where they are going.

Try this

Work in groups and brainstorm some ideas about train journeys. Here are some things to think about.

- What train journeys have you made? Where did you go? Why did you go?
- Have you read any good stories about train journeys? Who were the characters? What happened on the journey? How did the writer describe the journey? Where did the journey begin and end?

Make some notes as you talk about this.

HINT

Think carefully about the verb tenses that you will use in your story.

- For direct speech: use the present simple.
- For an event that is not finished or may be repeated: use the present perfect tense.
- For an event that is finished and in the past: use the past simple.
- For an event that happened while something else was happening: use the past continuous in one of the clauses.

CHALLENGE YOURSELF

Now work alone and plan, draft, edit and write your own story about a train journey. You can make this up or you can write about a real journey.

- Write 120–150 words.
- Use paragraphs.
- Use connectives to link your ideas.
- Include at least three sentences that include two clauses, one with past simple tense and one with past continuous tense, and one prepositional phrase.

Self check

- Did you use the correct verb tenses?
- Did you connect ideas with connectives?
- Did you check your spelling?

What can you do?

Read and review what you can do.

- I can listen to talks and conversations about travelling by train.
- I can talk about different types of train travel and experiences.
- I have read a blog about bullet trains and metros.
- I have read a story about a trip on a train.
- I can use prepositions in phrases with nouns and adjectives.
- I can use past continuous and present perfect forms to describe events.
- I can write a description of people and places on a train journey.

Now you have completed Unit 4, you may like to try the Unit 4 online knowledge test if you are using the Boost eBook.

5 The digital world

In this unit you will:
- listen to a conversation and a talk show about cyber safety
- speak about online safety and developing technology
- read short extracts and complete a multiple-choice questionnaire
- use noun phrases and modal forms
- express your opinions in writing.

Speaking and listening

Types of social media

 Working in a group, discuss the photograph of young people using social media.

1 What does 'social media' mean?
2 What do you especially like about this **medium**? Is there anything you don't like so much about it?
3 What social media apps are popular in your country?
4 What social media apps do your parents use?

Vocabulary

1 Match apps with the descriptions. Draw lines to connect the app name and the description. You could also go online and find the **logo** for each of these apps.

Snapchat	A scrapbooking app, where you can collect and display things that interest you
Instagram	A social networking site where you can share with friends and family online
Twitter	A photo-sharing app, where photos and videos (live stories) are available for a limited time only
Facebook	A comment app, where your posts are limited to a certain number of characters
Pinterest	A photo-sharing social networking site. You can also make stories from your photos

2 The noun 'media' is the plural form of 'medium'. It is an irregular form. Do you know the plural forms of these irregular nouns? Find the irregular plural for these singular words. Use each plural form in a sentence.

child	loaf	person	appendix	hoof
cactus	foot	mouse	shelf	

Try this

Work in a group. Here are three words that have been used in English for hundreds of years, but now have new meanings relating to the **digital** world. Discuss and then write a definition of the digital meanings for each of these words.

mouse	post	smart

Speaking and listening

Social media

Listen to Audio 5.1. The conversation is between a mother and her son about getting a smartphone.

1 Listen once and write down the reasons why the son wants a phone.
2 Then listen again. Why did the mother say 'no' at first? Write down one reason she gave.
3 Then listen for a third time. Write down what agreement the mother and the son reached about using the phone.

> **DID YOU KNOW?**
>
> **Phishing** refers to emails or text messages sent by criminals trying to obtain personal details such as passwords and bank details. The messages may look like they are from a trustworthy source to try and fool the reader.
> **'Catfishing'** is when a person uses a fake identity online, pretending to be someone else to trick other people.

PRACTISE

 Discuss the 'phishing' definition with a partner.

Write down your own definition for 'phishing'.

 Share your definition with the rest of the class. Who has the best definition?

> **LET'S TALK**
> Hold a class discussion about ways to stay safe from phishing when you are using social media.

> **LET'S TALK**
> Work in groups. Listen to the following conversations about modern technology in Audio 5.2. Then take turns to read each dialogue aloud.
>
> After you have read the dialogues, discuss the opinions that are expressed in each conversation.
>
> - Which statements do you agree with?
> - Which statements do you disagree with?
> - Make notes to summarise the opinions expressed in the conversations.
>
> - Would most of the people in the conversations agree or disagree with this statement: 'Mobile phones and the internet are essential parts of modern life?'

Conversation 1

Jasmine: I think we shouldn't be allowed to have phones at school. That way, if you don't have one, like me, you don't feel bad.

Rosa: No. I don't agree! I must have my phone.
What if my mum wants to call me? I have a phone, so I should be allowed to use it.

Conversation 2

Ben: The internet should be free to all citizens. It has to be a public service because we all need it.

May: I have to do a lot of research so I cannot do my assignments without the internet.

Ben: I need the internet on my phone and on my laptop. We have to hand in our assignments electronically as well.

Conversation 3

Elizabeth: These smartphones should never have been invented. They are terrible!

Daniel: I think they're very useful. You can do so many things with your phone. Let me show you.

Conversation 4

Salma: You are always on your phone!

Farah: My whole life is on my phone. I can't be without it! I would feel lost and cut off from the world.

Salma: You could try and have a phone-free day! It's quite nice.

Use of English

Modal verbs

Do you remember?

Words such as 'can', 'must' and 'may' are often used with other verbs. They tell us more about the other verbs. For example:

I can use a smartphone.

- The main verb is 'use'.
- The modal verb is 'can'. It tells us that the person is able to use the smartphone.

Modal verbs are helping words that we add to the main verb. They help us to express permission, obligation, advice, possibility or ability. Look at this table.

What the modal verbs express	Modal verbs
permission	can, could
obligation	must, have to
advice	should
possibility	might, may
ability	can, could

We can also use the negative 'not' with modal verbs. For example:

You cannot have a new phone this year.

You must not use all your data in one day!

He should not use his phone in the classroom.

We can also use modals in questions. For example:

Can/May I have a new phone, please?

Should I take my phone to school?

Try this

Work in pairs. Identify the modal verbs in each sentence.
1   My aunt and uncle can use the internet.
2   Please may I have more data for my phone?
3   You must be careful when you use social media.
4   My brother says I should not **post** photographs of myself on social media.

PRACTISE

Work in pairs. Choose the correct word to complete this dialogue. Read the dialogue aloud using the correct words. Then write the complete dialogue in your notebook.

Son: Please (may/must) I have your old smartphone?

Mother: Son, you (would/should) not have a phone; you are too young.

Son: But Mum, I (must/may) have a phone! Otherwise I will be left out!

Mother: Fine, you (can/may) have a phone, but you (would/should) keep your information private.

Son: Thank you, Mum! You (will/won't) ever regret this, I promise!

PRACTISE

Complete these sentences about digital technology, using the modal verbs from the box. Write your sentences in your notebook.

can	could	must	have to	should	might	may

1 You _____ always use a password that is hard to guess.
2 I _____ download some **software** to protect my information.
3 They _____ use the internet whenever they want to, it's not fair!
4 We _____ be able to log into the game, if we can get a connection.
5 You _____ use my computer, if you want.
6 _____ you please turn off your phones in class?
7 My brother says I _____ change my password every month.

PRACTISE

1 Listen carefully to the words that are emphasised in these sentences in Audio 5.3. Read them as you listen. Then repeat the sentences to your partner.
   a Please may I have a new computer for my birthday?
   b You should be very careful with your private information.
   c I can't find my new phone! Where could I have put it?
   d I have to bring my phone to school today because I need to contact my mother after school.

2 Now make five sentences of your own, using modal verbs from the box above. Practise reading your sentences to your partner.

LET'S TALK

Work in a group to present your own talk show. You will need:
- a talk show host
- an expert, who will answer questions
- at least two other people who will ask questions.

Choose a topic that you like from this list, or create your own topic.
- 'There should not be age restrictions on computer games.'
- 'Mobile phones should be allowed in classrooms.'
- 'Online bullying should be punishable by law.'

Prepare your talk show together, and then present it to the class.

Reading

Technological inventions

Read the table of inventions with a partner.
- Make a timeline on a big sheet of paper.
- Plot all of these events on your timeline.
- Which invention do you think has affected your life the most?
- What do you think might be invented in the next few years?

Year	Invention	Year	Invention
1712	Steam engine	1901	Radio
1814	Steam locomotive train	1903	Aircraft
1830	Photography	1926	Television
1868	Wristwatch	1942	Nuclear power
1876	Telephone	1946	Electronic computer
1878	Electric lightbulb	1957	Space rocket
1885	Petrol-driven car	1971	Pocket calculator; digital watch
		1975	Home computer
		1982	Compact-disc player

Looking at a website

Before you read the information on this website, read these questions carefully and discuss them in your groups.
1 Where would you click to find advice?
2 What do you think is in the Toolbox?
3 Discuss the information you can find on the Childline website.
4 Do you think the choice of pictures is good or not? Say why you think so.

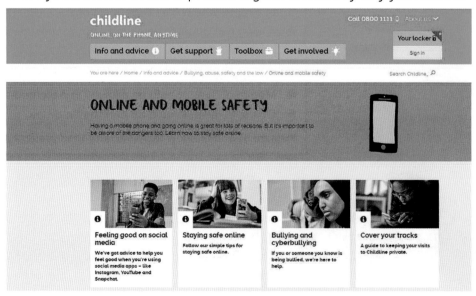

Read this short text about staying safe online.

Staying safe online

It is good practice for apps and websites to have safety advice and well-designed safety features which can make a real difference to how safe you will be when using them.

Make sure you understand the point of the safety and privacy features on your apps and how to use them. The tools are actually quite easy to manage.

Talk to your parents or carers about which social media apps you use and what you like about them. They might want to give them a try as well!

Learn how you can use privacy settings to make sure only your real friends and people you know can see your posts and images.

Make sure none of your apps have 'geo-location' enabled; these might mean you are accidentally sharing your location online.

Make sure you know how to report offensive comments or block people who upset you.

Check your 'tagging' settings to make sure that other people's posts will not reveal your identity. Always get other people's consent before sharing their photos online.

LET'S TALK

Use these questions to hold a discussion about online safety in your group.
1. Do all your apps have safety features?
2. Do you share with your parents what you are doing online?
3. What rules are there in your household about being online?
4. What privacy settings do you have on your device?
5. Is there any other advice you can think of that parents should be giving to their children?

In your group, make a short five-point summary of the advice you would give to other students about online safety.

- You can use ideas from the text, or your own ideas.
- How many groups have the same points?
- Present your five points to the rest of the class.

Vocabulary and spelling

1. Listen to these words in Audio 5.4, then practise saying them yourself. Where does the stress fall in each word?

internet	digital	media	scientist
feature	privacy	offensive	invention
computer	information	discovery	technology

2. Which words have three syllables? Which words have four? Try clapping out the rhythm of each word to test your answer.
3. Look at the jumbled up words. How many new words can you make out of joining up two of the words?

Use of English

Noun phrases

Do you remember?

Sentences need:
- a subject (the person doing the action)
- a verb (the action).

For example:

She plays games.

Peter won.

Most sentences also need:
- an object (the thing the action happens to).

For example:

They have smartphones.

The developer made a game.

The subject and object of a sentence are usually nouns.

You can replace the noun with a noun phrase.

A noun phrase is a group of words (without a verb) that makes sense.

For example:

The very fast **development** of digital technology is amazing.

People in the streets were queuing to be the first to buy the new smartphone.

HINT

If you are unsure if a group of words is a noun phrase, see if it answers the question 'who?' or 'what?' in connection with the verb. It helps to begin by underlining the verb in the sentence.

PRACTISE

Find the noun phrases in these sentences and write them in your notebook. The first one has been completed for you.

1 Everyone in the computer lab <u>shouted</u> when she won the game. (Who, or what <u>shouted</u>? <u>Everyone in the computer lab</u>)
2 Online games like Minecraft can be lots of fun.
3 Games can improve your **co-ordination**, problem-solving skills and multi-tasking skills.
4 You should read 'How to stay safe in a gaming environment'.
5 The placement of the computer in the house is important.
6 You must activate parental controls on the device.
7 Video chatting with grandparents is a safe use of technology.

PRACTISE

1 Work in pairs. Make up sentences using these noun phrases.
  a A huge amount of information on the internet …
  b Many young and inexperienced game players …
  c The parental control function of the game …
  d Your personal details, like your name and phone number …
  e Inventions like cameras and photography …

2 Choose one of the sentences you have made. Use it as a topic (main) sentence in a short presentation of three–five sentences (one paragraph) to your group or class. For example:

There is <u>a huge amount of information</u> on the internet these days. Some of the information is very useful and interesting, but some of it is disturbing as well. It is often difficult to decide what information is correct and what you should believe!

PRACTISE

Copy these sentences into your notebook and punctuate them correctly. Then underline the noun phrase in each sentence.

1 the mobile phone with a blue cover is mine

2 dont put any of your personal information online

3 my mum said remember not everyone is who they say they are

4 respect other peoples views even if you dont agree with them

5 think before you post videos photos or other personal bits of information

6 if you feel unsafe leave the website turn off your computer and talk to someone you trust

Try this

What do these emojis mean?

Speaking and listening

Talking about online safety

 Listen to Audio 5.5, which features a radio call-in show with an expert talking about staying safe online. As you listen, complete a mind map, like this one, about all the ways to stay safe online.

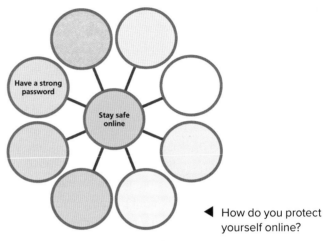

◄ How do you protect yourself online?

LET'S TALK

1 Discuss your mind maps in your group.
   a What else should you do to keep yourself safe online? Add your own ideas to your mind map.
   b Open the discussion to the whole class. Let a scribe, or the teacher, write all your ideas onto one mind map on the board so you have a summary of everything you have heard and discussed.
2 Talk about what Ms IT Lightley has to say in your group.
   a Do you agree with her advice that anything you post should be suitable for your grandmother to see?
   b What did caller 1 (Adam) do that was really silly?
   c What other advice would you give him?
   d What advice would you give to caller 2?

CHALLENGE YOURSELF

Play the 'Secure Online' game with a partner. Your teacher will give you a printout of the game to play. Read the instructions aloud. Can you be first to the finish line, using all you know about staying safe online?

You will need:
● a die
● two counters.

Roll the die to move forward. First one over the line wins!

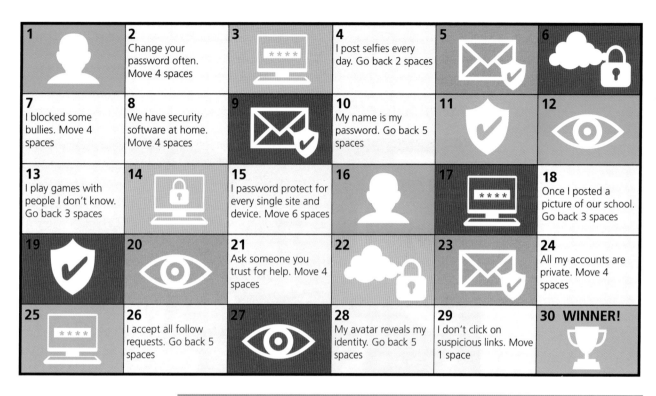

CHALLENGE YOURSELF

First, read the text messages on the mobile phone. Then 'translate' the messages into real sentences using the right words and write them out in your notebook.

Try this

Punctuate this text correctly.

in a mobile age children cant be completely protected even by the best privacy controls so its important to keep talking to your child about the implications of social media getting a sense of what they think is a useful place to start you may be surprised by how much thought they may have given to the issues **encourage** your child to think carefully about the way they and others behave online and how they might deal with difficult situations

Reading

Test yourself: are you safe?

Read this multiple-choice questionnaire about keeping yourself safe online when playing games.

● Read it first for the information.
● Choose your answers for each question.
● Then discuss your answers with a friend.

Activity

1 Online gaming:
   a builds social skills and co-ordination
   b creates a generation of zombies
   c is for people who have no friends.
2 The role of parents of gamers is to:
   a install **security** software to protect their children
   b allow open access to all online games
   c not interfere unless they are gamers themselves.
3 When choosing a screen name:
   a use a name that reflects your personality
   b always use an **avatar** that protects your real identify
   c choose one made out of one of your family or pets' names.

4 Children who play online games:
   a get obsessed with the game world and forget real life
   b know that it is just a game, like any other game
   c don't do as well at school as other children.
5 Some of the risks you run as a gamer include:
   a people accessing your image through your **web cam**
   b strangers trying to message you through **private messaging**
   c potential bullies or abusers contacting you through the game chat function
   d all of the above.

6 If you find a loot box in a game:
  a open it immediately, it may be treasure or extra power
  b open it immediately, it could be essential to progress in the game
  c approach with care, it could be a trap.
7 **Skins** that can disguise or alter your avatar:
  a can be used to gamble
  b can be converted to cash
  c are just part of the game.
8 If you are being bullied online:
  a block, **mute** or unfriend the abuser
  b turn off the in-game chat function
  c report the person to the game site administrator
  d all of the above.

9 How often should your parents allow you to buy extra content, like special powers, for a game?
  a Once a week
  b Once a month
  c On special occasions like birthdays
  d I buy my own extras.
10 Which of these are signs of too much gaming?
  a Tiredness and eye strain
  b Sunburn on the back of your neck and top of your hands
  c An inability to concentrate in class leading to worse grades at school.

Vocabulary

Read through the questionnaire again. Find the words in the box below in the questionnaire. Look at the sentences in which they occur. Use the sentences around the words to help you write down definitions for these terms.

avatar	chat	loot box	skin
web cam	mute	private messaging	

LET'S TALK

In the next lesson you are going to write a persuasive essay about one of the topics below. Work with a partner. Discuss any ideas you have around these topics.

Choose your topic now.
1 There should be no parental controls over how we use the internet – freedom of speech!
2 Games have to be age-restricted, otherwise small children could see very bad things.
3 The internet should only be accessible by people age 18 and over.

Writing

Expressing opinions

You are going to write an essay about internet safety. Remember, you have chosen one of the following topics:

1 There should be no parental controls over how we use the internet – freedom of speech!

2 Games have to be age-restricted, otherwise small children could see very bad things.

3 The internet should only be accessible by people age 18 and over.

Before you begin to write, read this short text about cyber security and the things you should and should not do to stay safe online. It will help you to revise some of the things you have read and talked about in this unit.

Stay safe online

You should not:
- post online a photo of your ID or your bank card, or of where you live or go to school.
- use a password that's easy to guess, like the name of your dad or your school.
- accept follow requests from people you don't know or haven't met.
- click on a message sent from an account that looks **suspicious**.

You should:
- keep your account settings on private.
- use a password with a mixture of upper case and lower case letters and with numbers and symbols in it, so it's not easy for a hacker to guess.
- remember that some accounts could be false. You have to always do your research before trusting someone online.
- always ask someone you trust for their opinion if you feel something is suspicious.

Look at the diagram about how to structure an essay. Use this structure to help you write your essay about internet safety.

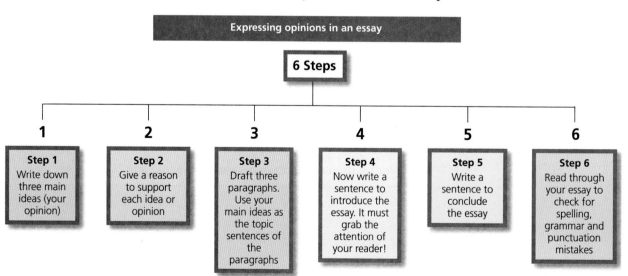

Expressing opinions in an essay

6 Steps

1	2	3	4	5	6
Step 1 Write down three main ideas (your opinion)	**Step 2** Give a reason to support each idea or opinion	**Step 3** Draft three paragraphs. Use your main ideas as the topic sentences of the paragraphs	**Step 4** Now write a sentence to introduce the essay. It must grab the attention of your reader!	**Step 5** Write a sentence to conclude the essay	**Step 6** Read through your essay to check for spelling, grammar and punctuation mistakes

PRACTISE

Now write your essay about internet safety. You should already have decided on your topic and the opinions you want to express. Here are some ideas that may help you.

- There should be no parental controls over how we use the internet. Freedom of speech!
- Games have to be age-restricted, otherwise small children could see very bad things.
- The internet should only be accessible by people age 18 and over.

Step 1: Write down your main ideas (your opinion). These will become the topic sentences of your paragraphs.

- Children spend far too much time on the internet.
- Children no longer know how to play.
- Children no longer know how to communicate with other people.

Step 2: Write a sentence to support each main idea.

Step 3: Now build your paragraphs. For example:

Children spend far too much time on the internet. They should be outside playing. You learn a lot by playing outside with other children. You learn to deal with other people, and to share. You cannot learn this by sitting in front of your computer.

Step 4: Now put together your essay.

- Start with an opening sentence. You can state a general opinion.
- Then add your three paragraphs.

Step 5: Write a conclusion to your essay.

Step 6: Ask a friend to proofread your essay. This means checking it to make sure:

- the meaning is clear
- punctuation is correct
- spelling and grammar are correct (pay attention to modal verbs!)
- your writing is neat and easy to read.

Once you have made any corrections, hand your completed essay to your teacher.

Self check

1 Use these noun phrases in sentences of your own.
  a Three very good pieces of evidence.
  b The dark, complicated world of the internet.
  c Age-restricted computer games.
  d The safety of your personal information.
  e A strong introductory paragraph.

2 Choose the correct modal verb to complete these sentences:
  a You (would/should) spend time outside, instead of playing computer games.
  b They (might/would) go to the internet café to play games.
  c We (should/could) join them there if you (would/could) like to.
  d This (may/can) be the last sentence in this unit.

What can you do?

Read and review what you can do.
- I can listen to a conversation and a talk show about cyber safety.
- I can speak about online safety and the speed of development of technology.
- I can read short extracts and a multiple-choice questionnaire.
- I can use noun phrases and modal forms.
- I can write my opinions in an essay.

 Now you have completed Unit 5, you may like to try the Unit 5 online knowledge test if you are using the Boost eBook.

6 Sports

In this unit you will:
- listen to discussions about **inclusivity** in sports
- listen to a panel discussion about which games to include in the Paralympic Games
- talk about inclusivity in sports
- read about new Olympic sports
- read biographies of baseball players
- use prepositions in phrases with idiomatic meanings
- use future forms to describe future events
- write an article about a sports event.

Speaking and listening

Talking about inclusivity

 1 Work in pairs. Look at the pictures on page 88 and answer the questions.
   a Can you name these sports?
   b Have you ever played any of these sports?
   c What do you need to play each sport?
   d Do you know anyone who plays each sport?
   e Do you think you will try these sports one day?

If you are not sure, read the names in this box and match them with the pictures on page 88.

rugby	judo	surfing	cricket
skateboarding	sprinting	wheelchair tennis	wheelchair racing

 2 What do you think 'inclusivity' in sport means? Read the 'Did you know?' box below, then listen to the students in Audio 6.1. They are talking about inclusivity in sport.

> **DID YOU KNOW?**
> Inclusivity means to include everyone and to treat everyone fairly and equally, no matter what their abilities, **gender**, **race**, **religion**, class or beliefs are. If you are not *included,* you are *excluded.* So, for example, if a person is a wheelchair user and a sports club does not provide wheelchair access, that person is excluded from the sports club. The sports club is not inclusive.

HINT
Look for photographs of people playing the sport. They may help you decide if the sport is inclusive or not.

Try this

Work in groups. Identify two or three sports or games that you think are inclusive. Answer the questions below for each of the sports. Give reasons for your answers.
1 What challenges do people with disabilities face?
2 Is expensive equipment needed to play the sport?
3 How can the sport be made more inclusive?
4 Could you play this sport?

HINT
When you give a reason for your answer, try to give real examples from your own experience and knowledge. If you know someone who is differently-abled, or if you are differently-abled yourself, think about how easy or how difficult surfing would be.

For example, 'I think surfing is a good sport for athletes who are differently-abled'.

Speaking and listening

Listen to a panel discussion

Before you listen to the panel discussion in Audio 6.2, look at the photographs below and read the captions.

▲ This young athlete is differently-abled. He uses his arms and a wheelchair to take part in a **race**

▲ This surfer is differently-abled. He has a **prosthetic** leg

LET'S TALK

What is your opinion? Do you think surfing should be included in the Paralympics?

● Is surfing inclusive?

● Will surfing **appeal** to young people?

● Can differently-abled athletes participate easily?

● Why is it difficult to judge surfing in a fair way?

PRACTISE

Listen again to the discussion in Audio 6.2 about the proposal to include surfing as a sport in the Paralympic Games. Then complete these sentences, using words from the box. Write the complete sentences in your notebook.

surfboard	ride	compete
appeal	encourage	waves

1 We need to _____ our youth to support the Paralympics.
2 Surfing will _____ to both young men and young women.
3 To compete, athletes will need a _____.
4 Differently-abled athletes can _____ in surfing events.
5 In the sea, _____ are never the same, which makes surfing difficult to judge fairly.
6 The proposal suggests that athletes _____ 25 waves.

PRACTISE

The International Paralympic Committee (IPC) has confirmed that the next Paralympic Games sports programme will include the following 14 sports:

athletics	wheelchair badminton	shooting
wheelchair tennis	judo	sitting volleyball
swimming	cycling	table tennis
archery	rowing	wheelchair basketball
wheelchair rugby	goalball	

Listen to the words in Audio 6.3 as you read them. Then practise saying them aloud. Listen to the word stress in each word. Which syllable do you need to stress?

Try this

Which sports do you think the symbols below represent? Say the names.

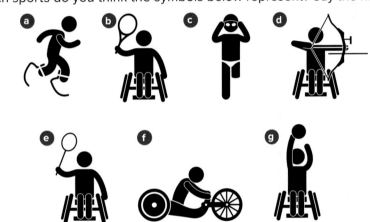

▲ Powerchair football team in action

LET'S TALK

Some people think that wheelchair football (also known as powerchair football) should be included in the Paralympic Games. What do you think? Have a short class debate about this.

● Your teacher will divide the class into two groups.
● One group will present two reasons why it would be a good idea to include wheelchair football.
● The other group will present two reasons why it would not be a good idea to include this sport.
● Each group should have about five minutes to present their ideas.
● Then have a class vote to decide which arguments are the most convincing.

Use of English

Expressions with prepositions

Prepositions are very useful words and we often use them to make phrases with special meanings – which makes them a bit tricky too!

Do you remember?

Prepositions describe location, time and direction. We can also use prepositions after adjectives to make phrases. For example:

I am happy with my choice.

We also often use prepositions with verbs to make expressions. It may be difficult to understand the meaning of these expressions, even if you know what each word in the expression means. Look at these examples:

I have tried to skateboard, but I just can't do it. So I give up!

To 'give up' means to 'stop trying'.

She's going to try out for the volleyball team.

In this sentence, to 'try out' means 'to test' to see if a person is good enough to join the team.

PRACTISE

Work in pairs. Read these sentences and look at the underlined phrases. What do you think they mean? Choose the correct meaning (a or b) under each sentence. Then check in a dictionary to see if you are correct.

1   We will not put up with sports clubs that are not inclusive. Boys and girls must be allowed to play the same sports.
    a   Tolerate   b   Understand

2   I never walk away from problems. I always try and deal with them.
    a   Ignore   b   Take a walk

3   Jodie looks after her little brother in the afternoons while her mum goes running.
    a   Care for   b   Look at

4   Athletes from all over the world will take part in the next Olympic Games.
    a   Party   b   Participate

5   Have you come across a sport called Taekwondo? What is it?
    a   Make a cross on   b   Heard about

6   Hold on, I don't agree! It is not fair to have games in which girls cannot compete!
    a   Put your hand on the handle   b   Wait

Try this

Work in small groups. Listen to the conversations in Audio 6.4. Then use prepositions to complete the phrases in these short conversations.

Practise the conversations in pairs. Try to use the correct intonation when you do this. Listen to the conversations again and take note of which word or words in each sentence are emphasised before you do this.

Meera: Come _____. Let's play some football.

Paulo: OK. But we need to warm _____ first.

Anief: Of course. We don't want to hurt ourselves. I'll show you what to do.

Lara: OK. And will you show us how to cool _____ afterwards too?

Anief: Of course! Let's go.

Meera: Have you ever come _____ a sport called badminton?

Paulo: Of course. It's an Olympic sport. My parents take part _____ the local championships every year. I join _____ sometimes too.

Anief: It's a bit like tennis, you hit something over a net. But the equipment is different.

Lara: Yes. I tried _____ for the local badminton team once but I wasn't good enough!

CHALLENGE YOURSELF

Use the following phrases in sentences of your own. Your sentences should describe an athlete or a sport.

look after	take part in	try out	put up with

Give your sentences to a partner to read. Discuss the sentences and agree on how to improve them.

Reading

Read an article from a sports magazine

1 Before you read this article, read the title and look at the photographs. What do you think the article is about?

New Olympic Sports

At the next Summer Olympics, 3×3 and Freestyle BMX will become official Olympic sports. The International Olympic Committee believes that sports like these will become more and more popular in the future. They also believe the sports will attract young people to the Games. They are going to introduce more new sports in 2024 and 2028.

3×3 Basketball

▲ A 3×3 basketball court in Japan

One of the most popular games in the world is 3×3 (we say 'three on three' or 'three by three'). People started playing this game on the streets of towns and cities, which is why it is sometimes called Streetball.

Men and women from many countries will compete in this new Olympic sport.

The game is similar to basketball because the aim is to put a ball into a basketball **hoop**. But in 3×3 there are only three players in each team at a time. Each team has a fourth player in reserve. There is also only one basketball hoop, so both teams use the same hoop. The game is very short. Each game lasts 10 minutes.

People predict that this game will be a huge attraction at future Olympic Games.

Freestyle BMX

The Olympic Committee believes that there will be more and more interest in **extreme** sports. Extreme sports are sports that are exciting to watch but also dangerous and require a high level of skill. Freestyle BMX riding is one of the new extreme sports that will become a permanent sport at the Olympic Games.

In future Olympic Games, riders will perform **tricks** on BMX bicycles on different

surfaces. Some riders prefer smooth, flat surfaces (called 'flatland'). These riders will do tricks such as 'wheelies' and 'endos' with only one wheel of the bike on the ground.

Other riders will perform on specially built vert ramps or on hard dirt **trails**. Riders who ride on dirt trails will perform tricks such as 'tabletop' and 'the superman' with their bodies up in the air as they ride. They hold on to the **handlebars** of the BMX bikes as they do this.

It's going to be very exciting to watch!

▲ A BMX freestyle rider doing tricks on a vert ramp

2 Discuss and answer these questions.
  a Why did the International Olympic Committee add new sports to the Olympic Games? Give two reasons.
  b Which game is easier to play on a street, traditional basketball or 3×3 basketball? Why?
  c Are 3×3 and freestyle BMX inclusive sports? Give one reason.
  d Why do you think freestyle BMX is called an 'extreme' sport?
  e How do freestyle BMX riders do tricks?
  f Would you like to take part in either of these sports? Give a reason.

Vocabulary and spelling

PRACTISE

1 Listen to these words in Audio 6.5, then say them aloud.

Olympic Games	official	popular
extreme	tournament	trick

2 Answers to these questions can be found using the words in the box above.
  a This word means something that a lot of people like.
  b These take place every four years.
  c The opposite of this word is 'unofficial'.
  d A 'wheelie' is an example of this.
  e This means dangerous, not average or usual.
  f This word means a competition in which people play games or sports.

3 Learn to spell these words. First read each word, then cover it with your hand and write the word in your notebook. Work with a partner to practise writing the words again.

CHALLENGE YOURSELF

Work with a partner and find out about another extreme sport. Make notes about:
● Where do people play or practise this sport (on land or on water or in the air)?
● The equipment needed for the sport.
● Why is it called an 'extreme' sport?
● Whether or not it is an Olympic sport.

Report back to the class.

Use of English

Talking about the future?

Do you remember?

We can express the future in different ways. Look at these examples:

3×3 basketball is <u>going to be</u> a sport at the next Olympic Games.

(Use going to + verb stem to describe plans and arrangements that have already been made.)

The sport <u>will appeal</u> to young people.

(Use will + verb stem to make predictions.)

The 2024 Paris Olympics <u>start</u> on Friday 26 July 2024.

(Use the present tense to describe future arrangements with fixed dates.)

PRACTISE

Copy these sentences into your notebook and underline the parts of the sentences that express the future.

1 Are you going to watch the Olympic Games on television tomorrow? No, I don't think I will have the time.

2 We won't be able to attend the games unfortunately.

3 Which way are we going? Can you show me the way, please?

4 What time is the surfing event tomorrow? It's going to be very exciting to watch!

Try this

Work in pairs. Use the words below to make sentences and questions about the future. You can add words and change the form of the verbs.

1 Freestyle BMX (to appeal) to young people.

2 Where the 2024 Olympic Games (to take place)?

3 Which event (to be) the most exciting?

4 The match (to start) at 6:30 p.m. on Saturday evening.

5 The riders (to perform) tricks on the vert ramp.

6 The International Olympic Committee (to introduce) new sports in 2028.

Copy the completed sentences into your notebook.

PRACTISE

Listen to the intonation in these sentences in Audio 6.6. Which words are emphasised? Then practise the sentences in pairs, using the same intonation.

1   They hope the sport will appeal to people in many different countries.
2   The new basketball game 3×3 is going to be very popular at the Olympic Games.
3   We won't be able to watch that match tonight.
4   Will our team win the match next week?

CHALLENGE YOURSELF

IWork in groups. Do some research about the next Olympic and Paralympic Games. Choose two sports that interest your group. Find out who the best athletes in each sport are and the country from which they come. Then discuss and predict who will win gold, silver and bronze medals.

Give reasons for your answers.

Report back to the class with your predictions.

	GOLD MEDAL	SILVER MEDAL	BRONZE MEDAL
MEN'S TENNIS	Dominic Thiem (Austria)	Stephanos Tsitsipas (Greece)	Felix Auger-Aliassime (Canada)
WOMEN'S 50 METRE FREESTYLE SWIMMING	Li Guizhi (China)	Michelle Konkoly (USA)	Aurélie Rivard (Canada)

Speaking and listening

Draw up a proposal

Try this

It is your turn to make a proposal about new games to be included in the Olympics or the Paralympics. You have discussed this already. Now you need to convince others about a new sport.

Work in groups. Draw up a proposal for one new sport. In your proposal you should:
- explain what the sport is (What do athletes do? Where do they play?)
- state your opinion about why this sport should be included (Is it entertaining to watch? Is it popular?)
- give three good reasons to support your opinion.

Present your proposal to the class. This should take no more than five minutes. Be short and clear!

HINT

Give examples and evidence to support your opinions. Try to find factual information such as statistics. For example:
- How many people in your country play this sport?
- How many clubs in the country play the sport?
- How many people watch it on television?
- Is the sport equally popular with men and women?
- Do young people play this sport?

HINT
- Did you use the ideas and vocabulary from this unit?
- Did you use the future tense where necessary?
- Did you support your opinion with factual reasons?

CHALLENGE YOURSELF

Do your presentation as a poster or on a computer. Include photographs of the sport as well.

Reading

Read biographies of famous baseball players

LET'S TALK

Before you read, talk about baseball with your class and try to find answers to these questions.
1   Do you play baseball?
2   Do you know what *a pitcher, a batter* and *a catcher* do in baseball?
3   What do you need to play baseball?
4   What does a baseball field look like?
5   Do you know what the NL is?

Try this

1   Look at the photographs on the next page. Which baseball players will you read about? Which one of them is a pitcher and which one is a batter? Write down your answers and check them after you have read the text.
2   Read the biographies. Make a note of any words you do not understand.

DID YOU KNOW?

Baseball is very popular in many countries, but the United States of America has the most famous baseball league, the National League (NL). Many players in other countries dream about going to play baseball for one of the famous teams in the USA.

Albert Pujols

Albert Pujols or to give him his full name, José Alberto Pujols Alcántara, is a famous baseball player from the USA. He has played for teams such as the St Louis Cardinals and the Angels.

Albert Pujols was born in the Dominican Republic in 1980. He moved to the USA 16 years later where he played baseball at college. He was signed by the Cardinals and in 2001 was voted the 'Rookie of the Year' in the first year that he played in the National League. He went on to play in two World Series Championships.

Pujols bats (hits) and pitches (throws) with his right hand. He is quite tall at 1.91 m (6 ft 3 in) and he weighs around 107 kg (235 lb). His skill as a batter has won him the title of 'Silver Slugger' several times, scoring more than 600 home runs and more than 3000 hits in his career.

Pujols will retire soon but people will celebrate his amazing skills in baseball and he will join the baseball Hall of Fame.

Yusei Kikuchi

Yusei Kikuchi is an up-and-coming baseball player. People predict that he will become a major baseball star in the USA. He was born in 1991 and played for the Saitama Seibu Lions in the Nippon Professional Baseball (NPB) League in Japan. Later he signed with the Melbourne Aces in the Australian Baseball League (ABL), before joining the Seattle Mariners in the Major League Baseball (MLB) in the USA for four years.

All the major NPB teams in Japan were keen to sign this exciting young left-handed pitcher. Many US teams were interested in signing him too, but he decided to become a professional in Japan first before moving to the USA.

Kikuchi is 1.82 m (6 ft) and weighs about 88 kg (194 lb). He is left-handed and is able to throw many different types of balls successfully. At high school he once threw a fastball that was recorded at 154 km/h (96 mph)! Although one thing that Kikuchi has not done yet is hit a home run – maybe he will add this to his list of successes in the future too. He is definitely someone to watch!

Try this

Write your answers to these questions.

1 In which country was Albert Pujols born?
2 Where did Yusei Kikuchi first begin to play baseball?
3 Albert Pujols has earned two important titles. Write down the names of the titles. Can you explain what each name means? Look for clues in the text.
4 True or false?
   a Albert Pujols once played for the Saitama Seibu Lions.
   b Yusei Kikuchi will probably become a very famous baseball player.
5 Why did many US baseball teams want to sign Yusei Kikuchi?
6 What is the baseball Hall of Fame? Why will Albert Pujols become a member?

Vocabulary and spelling

PRACTISE

1 Find words in the text which have the same or similar meanings.
   a To bat
   b To throw
   c An organisation in which teams compete against each other
   d A person who earns money from playing a sport

 2 Work in pairs. Look at the underlined expressions in each sentence in this paragraph and discuss what each means. Then share your ideas with the class.

> Yusei Kikuchi is an <u>up-and-coming</u> baseball player. He <u>signed with the Melbourne Aces</u> in the Australian Baseball League (ABL) and then he <u>went on</u> to play in the USA. He is definitely <u>someone to watch</u>!

3 Listen to these sentences in Audio 6.7 as you read them. Learn to spell the underlined words.

> She is a <u>baseball</u> <u>player</u> who plays in the national <u>league</u> in the USA. She has <u>signed</u> with a well-known team in the USA. People say she will become a <u>famous</u> <u>pitcher</u>.

4 Make your own sentences with each of the spelling words.

CHALLENGE YOURSELF

Work in pairs. Find out about another famous baseball player. Find a photograph of the player and write down five interesting pieces of information about the player. Tell your group about the player or make a short presentation to the class.

Writing

Write a sports article

Most of us watch some sport and sometimes we read reviews about sports matches. Read the following review about an Olympic sports event held in Rio de Janeiro in 2016. Look up any words that you do not understand. Read the annotations which will help you to understand the structure of the review.

The first paragraph gives the essential information that the reader needs: Who? What? Where? When?

This paragraph gives more information about the event.

This paragraph states an opinion and gives a prediction as a conclusion.

A first gold for Singapore!

I am lucky enough to be at the Olympic Games. Tomorrow I am going to watch a race that I think I will remember for many years. I will see Joseph Schooling from Singapore as well as the great Michael Phelps, Chad le Clos and Laszlo Cseh in the men's 100 m butterfly final swimming event.

It will be close and very exciting. Schooling has broken many records back home in Singapore, but maybe he will win a gold medal this time. If he does, it will be the first gold medal to be won by Singapore at the Olympic Games. What a proud moment that will be!

Schooling said it 'will be a dream come true' if he does win. He also says that he and his team have worked very, very hard to get a medal. I think this talented young man will become one of the stars of the future.

◀ This article was written before the race – and yes, Schooling did win a gold medal!

Try this

Now plan, draft, edit and write an article of a match or game or sports event that you are going to watch. Your article should have three or four paragraphs (about 150 words). State your opinion about the event quite clearly and give reasons why you think this way. Remember to link your ideas.

HINT

Draft your article and give it to a friend to read. Let your friend suggest how you can improve it. For example, did you give your reader all the important information in the first paragraph? Without this information the reader will not be able to understand the review.

Remember to check your spelling!

CHALLENGE YOURSELF

Write an article in which you express a different opinion about a sports event. For example, you may believe that one athlete or team should have won a gold medal for their performance. Perhaps they were unlucky?

Self check

Did you check your use of future forms? Read the notes on page 96 again if you are unsure.

What can you do?

Read and review what you can do.
- I can listen to discussions about sports and understand the main ideas.
- I understand what inclusivity in sport is and why it is important.
- I can read biographies.
- I can write a review of a sports match.
- I use and understand future forms.
- I know how to work out the meanings of new expressions and can use some of them myself.

 Now you have completed Unit 6, you may like to try the Unit 6 online knowledge test if you are using the Boost eBook.

PRACTISE

Use prepositions to complete the following sentences.

1   She will be a passenger _____ (in/on) the fast train to London.

2   Dylan and Pete are going _____ (to/on) holiday _____ (with/by) their family next month.

3   I need the internet _____ (by/on) my phone and my laptop.

4   I work _____ (about/out) at the gym twice a week.

5   Teams from all over the world take part _____ (on/in) the Paralympic Games.

6   Sarah does not put up _____ (of/with) rude people on the train.

7   'I give _____ (over/up)!' said my gran. 'I don't know how to use this smartphone.'

8   Have you come _____ (about/across) the word 'catfishing'? Do you know what it means?

9   Mara is quite happy _____ (with/by) the new software on the computer. She says it makes things much easier.

10 It can be difficult to get _____ (around/over) if the trains are not running.

> **Try this**

Read the texts. Then use words from the box to complete the paragraphs.

extreme	dangerous	tricks	passengers
online	reflect	personal	handlebars
download	journeys	bullet	unfollow

1   I have always loved train _____. I enjoy all types of trains – underground, _____ trains and steam trains. I think I enjoy them because I always travel by train when I am on holiday. I have time to relax and _____ on things. I watch the other _____ and sometimes listen to music too.

2   We put ourselves at risk when we go _____. So how can we stay safe? Here are a few tips:

   a   Don't give out any _____ information.

   b   Block or _____ people who make rude comments on social media.

   c   Be careful what you _____. Only use safe websites.

3   More and more people take part in _____ sports. Extreme sports are sports that are exciting but also _____ , for example freestyle BMX riding. In this sport, riders perform _____ on one wheel only or up in the air. They hold on tight to the _____ when they do these tricks.

PRACTISE

Choose the correct verbs to complete each sentence.

1 My sister and I (were waiting/have waited) at the train station when the accident happened.

2 Lee (has never been/is never be) to London. Have you been there?

3 (Should/May) I have a new phone please, Mum?

4 You (must not/have not to) use all your data in one day!

5 What time (will be/is) the basketball match tomorrow? It's (going to be/will going to be) very exciting!

6 The sport (will go to/will) appeal to young people.

7 Have you ever (to see/seen) such a crowded railway station!

8 The last time Mount Vesuvius (was erupting/erupted) was in 1944.

LET'S TALK

Work in pairs and make noun phrases with these words. Then use each noun phrase in a sentence.

1 internet lots information

2 details personal

3 online games

4 parental controls device

5 everyone computer room

PRACTISE

Look at the photograph and complete the paragraph below using connectives. There are some ideas in the word box, but you will need to choose the best connective for each sentence.

as	but	while	that
because	and	although	

I looked out of the window _____ I was sitting on the train. The train was moving slowly _____ we were travelling up a steep mountain _____ it was raining _____ I could still see quite clearly. Some people were chatting, _____ others were sleeping. _____ the train carried on its way _____ more people started to fall asleep the carriage became so quiet _____ I could hear the rain on the windows.

CHALLENGE YOURSELF

Write a short story about one of these topics.

● Now I make sure that I am careful when I go online.

● That journey was the best trip I have ever made.

● Next year I am going to …

7 Success stories

In this unit you will:

- listen to a podcast about a successful entrepreneur
- find specific information and details during a listening exercise
- talk about success and the future, using the correct verb forms
- read aloud fluently, and read an interview and short texts about successful people
- use a range of noun and verb forms, including gerunds and the infinitive
- write a short paragraph and a business plan.

success – noun [uncountable] the fact that you have achieved something that you want and have been trying to do or get

For example:
- The new game has been a huge success in the market.

- At the start, our soccer club had a fair amount of success.

- I didn't have much success in finding the answer I was looking for.

success: getting the results you wanted or hoped for

For example:
- The success of a team depends on how people work together.

- Our group project was a big success!

- Both films have been big box-office successes.

- That salmon dish was a success, wasn't it?

Source: www.oxfordlearnersdictionaries.com

▲ Malala Yousafzai is the youngest winner of the Nobel Peace Prize. You will find out more about her later in this unit

▲ Billie Eilish was chosen to sing the song for a James Bond movie at only 18 years old!

Speaking and listening

What is success?

Do you remember?

Success is an abstract noun. Abstract nouns are nouns that you cannot see or feel or touch, such as:

joy	hope	fear
fun	**achievement**	

Try this

Use the abstract nouns from the box above to complete these sentences.

1 Going to the beach in summer is so much _____.

2 My sister's greatest _____ has been getting her driver's licence.

3 Sometimes, _____ holds me back from doing something, in case I fail.

4 The refugees live in _____ that they will soon get housing.

5 Dancing brings me so much _____, that I would like to do it as my job one day.

1 What is success? Success might mean different things to different people. Talk about this in your group. Use the ideas from the diagram to help you.

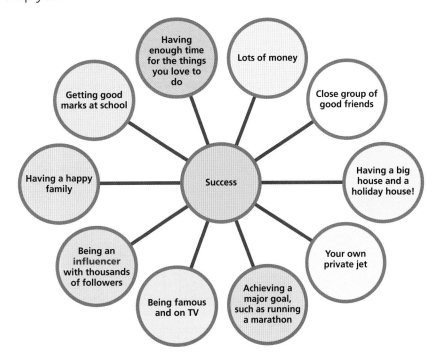

Having enough time for the things you love to do

Lots of money

Getting good marks at school

Close group of good friends

Having a happy family

Success

Having a big house and a holiday house!

Being an influencer with thousands of followers

Your own private jet

Being famous and on TV

Achieving a major goal, such as running a marathon

2 Work with a partner. Read the two dictionary definitions on page 106.
   a Which one do you think describes 'success' the best?
   b Choose two of the example sentences from the definitions that you like best. Write the two sentences in your notebook.

CHALLENGE YOURSELF

Look at the photographs below and read the captions. In your opinion, which of these two people do you think is the most successful? Write three sentences to explain why you think so.

◀ Greta Thunberg successfully **campaigned** against **climate change** while still a teenager

◀ Chadwick Boseman starred in the movie *Black Panther*, which introduced the world to one of the first black action heroes

Speaking and listening

Successful people

1 Listen to a conversation between two friends in Audio 7.1.
2 Discuss these statements in your group. Which opinion do you agree with? Which do you disagree with?
   a Maria measures success by how many things you have.
   b Jose thinks success is achieving something you set out to do.
   c Success is measured in terms of money or wealth.
   d Achievement is a better measure of success than money.
3 Does the rest of your group agree with you?
4 Which of the two people in the photographs would you most like to meet? Say why.

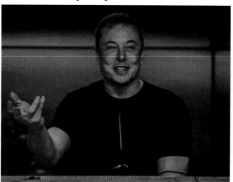

▲ Elon Musk invented an electric car called the Tesla

▲ Bill Gates started Microsoft – the operating system almost everyone in the world uses on their computers

Vocabulary

1 Read the table below. Then match each of the idiomatic words and phrases in the first column to its meaning in the second column. Write your own table in your notebook, with the meanings in the correct place.

Idiomatic word/phrase	Meaning
Bling	From a poor family
Filthy rich	A false name used by a writer to protect their identity
Oodles of dineros	Make something go up quickly
Pen name	Stopped a course of study
Scam	Lots of cash money
Tune in	Extremely and excessively rich
Cause a spike in	A trick played on someone to steal their money
From humble roots	Turn on a device so that you can listen to or watch a person or programme
Dropped out	Lots of very sparkly jewellery

HINT

These words come from the audio you just listened to, and the reading text and audios in the next few lessons. It will make your reading easier if you understand these terms.

2 Use five of the expressions from question 1 in sentences of your own. Compare your sentences with your partner's. Help each other to correct spelling and grammar mistakes.

3 Build new words with these abstract nouns, the prefix 'un' and the suffixes 'ful' and 'ly'.

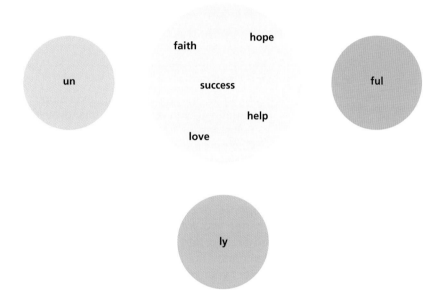

4 Use the correct form of the word in brackets to complete these sentences.
   a She practised the piano (faith) every day.
   b We had a (love) time learning all about teamwork on our summer camp.
   c His father is a (success) entrepreneur.
   d Being (hope) is what keeps me going – I know I'm going to win one day!

 5 In the next lesson you are going to be reading texts aloud. You will be reading about these three people:
   ● Greta Thunberg
   ● Malala Yousafzai
   ● DanTDM

Discuss what you know about these people in your group.
   a How have they been successful?
   b Why do you think they all appear in this unit?
   c Which person interests you most? Can you say why?

6 Make short notes about what you already know about these people. There is some information on the previous pages. Make a word spider diagram for each of the people.

Reading short texts

Different kinds of success

1 In this lesson we're going to practise reading short texts aloud. Read the helpful tips in this box with your partner.

DID YOU KNOW?

Here are some tips when reading texts aloud:
- Punctuation gives you clues and shows you how to breathe.
  - Full stops indicate you need to pause and breathe.
  - Commas mean you should take a slight pause.
  - A question mark means your voice should go slightly upwards at the end of the sentence.
- Vary your pace – the speed at which you read. Read slowly to build suspense, or quickly when there is a lot of action.
- Change your intonation – the pitch of your voice – speak higher when you are excited, and lower if the action is slow, or you want to build suspense.
- Remember the audience – make eye contact when there is a pause, project your voice so that everyone can hear you and use gestures to make the reading interesting.

---

 2 Choose one of the three short texts below. Practise reading the extract aloud to your partner. Take turns to correct one another's reading. Give each other a star rating based on:
- pausing in the right places
- varying your pace
- using the correct intonation
- making eye contact with your audience.

Five stars is very good, while one star means you need more practice.

Malala Yousafzai

Malala Yousafzai is a young woman from Swat Valley, Pakistan. She is passionate about education for girls. She wrote articles for the BBC Urdu programme about life under the Taliban. She often spoke about her family's fight for girls' education in her community.

In October 2012, Malala was shot when she was returning from school on a bus. She miraculously survived and continues her campaign for education.

In recognition of her **courage** and **bravery**, Malala was awarded the Nobel Peace Prize in 2014, becoming the youngest ever winner at just seventeen years old.

Greta Thunberg

Greta started planning her school strike over the summer of 2018. Her class at school had recently watched a movie about how much plastic there was in the ocean. There is an **island** of plastic, larger than Mexico, floating around in the South Pacific Ocean. This had a huge **impact** on Greta, and she began doing more research on how humans were damaging the planet.

Greta's father helped her to make a sign saying 'School strike for climate', and then on 28 August 2018, she got up, had breakfast and instead of cycling to school, cycled to the Swedish parliament, where she set up her board and a small pile of leaflets.

People started taking photographs, then someone posted on Twitter about her school strike for climate change; it got retweeted and a **film crew** arrived.

Some people stopped to question her and talk, and others began to join her sitting outside parliament. On the last day of her school strike, over a thousand people joined her. Journalists from various television programmes reported live from outside parliament. Greta had succeeded in bringing climate change to the world's attention. Has she done enough? Greta doesn't think so. She is continuing her campaign to make people aware.

DanTDM

Imagine doing what you love, and being a multi-millionaire before you are even 30 years old. In just one year, Dan Middleton earned more than most Hollywood actors and international sports stars do. So how did he do it?

At 22, Dan had graduated from university and was working in a supermarket. He started making videos in his spare time, first about Pokémon and then about Minecraft. He posted his first video to YouTube in 2012, when he created a gaming channel called 'The Diamond Minecart', and just two years later he had over 2.5 million subscribers to his channel.

As the popularity of his videos increased, Dan started making money from the advertising generated by people flocking to watch his channel. After a few years, he renamed the channel DanTDM. In his videos, Dan talks to his followers about how to play the games, discussing characters and game scenarios as well as sharing hints and tips. DanTDM takes a very responsible attitude to online posts. He has good advice to share with everyone.

DanTDM is now rated as one of the most popular YouTubers in the world. He has more than 23 million subscribers, and more than 17 billion video views. Now that's a lot!

CHALLENGE YOURSELF

Prepare a short presentation about another successful person that you find inspiring. Practise your presentation in front of the mirror at home or ask a family member to listen to you. Be ready to do your presentation in class.

Use of English

What do you want to be?

Do you remember?

The infinitive form of a verb is a verb that has 'to' in front of it.

PRACTISE

Can you identify the infinitive forms in these sentences?

1 He wants to be a millionaire.

2 She wants to play professional tennis.

3 He goes to see a private coach.

4 They want to learn Spanish.

PRACTISE

1 Add the infinitive form of the verb in brackets to complete these sentences.
   a Malala continues (fight) for access to education.
   b She used (ride) the bus home from school.
   c She likes (help) those in need.
   d She used (talk) on the radio.
   e Organisations want (assist) her with her mission.

2 Now use words from the box to complete these sentences.
   a Her aim is _____ the title before she turns sixteen.
   b What do you want _____ when you finish school?
   c My parents want me _____ an engineer, but I want _____ an animal nurse.
   d There is enough time in life _____ your ambitions.
   e That young boy is going _____ at whatever he tries to do!
   f I need _____ some more experience, before I apply to do the certificate.

to be	to achieve	to succeed	to do
to win	to become	to gain	

Try this

Correct the grammar errors in these sentences.

1 DanTDM to earn more than most Hollywood actors.

2 He never even have leave the house!

3 I want make money by playing games on the internet!

4 If you want be a success, you have work hard.

5 He to make a lot of money from advertising.

6 He used work in a supermarket.

Try this

Write a short paragraph about what you want to do in the future. Use this writing frame as a guide.

I want to be _____.

I want to go _____.

To do this I have to learn _____.

Finally, I want to be _____!

Vocabulary

HINT

I shall, we shall

All the rest will!

Do you remember?

To make the future tense, add shall or will to the main verb. For example:

I shall be famous!   They will buy tickets to see your shows.

You can also use the verb 'to be' + 'going to'. For example:

I am going to rule the world!   We are going to be there later.

PRACTISE

Choose the correct form of the verb in brackets to complete the sentences.

1   They (shall/will) go to the theatre tonight.

2   She (shall/will) become famous before she's thirty!

3   We (shall/will) be there just before eight o'clock.

4   Who (shall/will) we be meeting outside the venue?

5   When (shall/will) the conductor be arriving?

Try this

Talk to your partner about what you want to be in the future. Are you going to be an explorer? A computer scientist? A fantastic parent? You are going to play a game called 'twenty questions'. Write your chosen role on a piece of paper, for example, 'I am going to be a space explorer' and fold it up. Work with your partner to think up questions you can ask another pair to guess what they want to be in the future. You should use infinitive forms in your questions and make sure the questions can only be answered with 'yes' or 'no'.

Ask your questions to try to guess what they want to be in the future. The other pair then ask you and your partner questions to try to guess what each of you want to be.

Word	Synonym
en*tre*preneur	growth
inno*va*tion	newness
deve*lop*ment	surroundings
en*vir*onment	group
com*mun*ity	businessperson

The table contains five useful words to learn to spell. You will need them for the podcasts in the next lesson.

1   Say the words out loud, putting the emphasis on the correct syllable.

2   Match the words with the synonyms in the table.

3   Learn to spell the words.

Speaking and listening

Inspirational talks

1 There are lots of inspirational talks by successful people online. Listen to Audio 7.2, which introduces five people who have given talks on a variety of topics.

    a Which of these speakers would you like to listen to?

    b Why does this speaker's talk sound interesting?

    c Does your partner want to listen to the same talk? Why or why not?

> **HINT**
> Can you find the five useful words you learned for your spelling test in the previous lesson?

1	Cameron Herold: 'Let's raise kids to be entrepreneurs'
2	Maya Penn: 'Meet a young entrepreneur, cartoonist, designer, activist'
3	Nirmalya Kumar: 'India's invisible **innovation**'
4	Majora Carter: 'Three stories of local eco-entrepreneurship'
5	Simon Sinek: 'How great leaders inspire action'

◀ Simon Sinek discusses why some companies are more successful than others

2 If you have access to the internet, search for one of these inspirational talks to listen to in your group.

> Try this

Work in your group. Listen while your teacher plays Audio 7.2 again and then answer these questions.

  1 What does Cameron Herold believe?

  2 What four jobs does Maya Penn have?

  3 Where is Nirmalya Kumar from?

  4 Which is most important to Majora Carter? Choose one of these words: entrepreneurship, environment.

  5 Who makes the decisions, according to Simon Sinek?

Listen to a podcast

 1 Find out more about the YouTube sensation DanTDM. You will remember him from the earlier lessons. Listen to the podcast in Audio 7.3.

 2 Now listen as your teacher plays the podcast in Audio 7.3 a second time. Work with a partner. Try and find this specific information in the podcast. Choose from the selection shown in brackets.

    a DanTDM used to work in a supermarket as a (checkout operator / cleaner / shelf stacker).

    b He started making videos when he was (20 / 22 / 32).

    c His real name is (Dan Middleton / Dan Milton / Dan Mennington).

    d His channel is on (TikTok / Instagram / YouTube).

    e He makes money through (advertising / shelf stacking / teaching).

    f He has more than (17 billion / 22 million / 23 million) subscribers.

    g When he started making videos, Dan had just finished (school / university / training camp).

    h Dan talks to his followers about (working in a supermarket / making videos / how to play the games).

    i He has had more than (17 million / 70 million / 17 billion) video views on his channel.

Use of English

Sporting success

Try this

1 Find out the meaning of these abstract nouns. Look them up in the dictionary. Then write down their meaning. Learn to spell the words.

courage	kindness	friendship
success	achievement	love

2 Now use the abstract nouns in the box in sentences of your own.
3 Use the correct form of the verb in brackets to complete these sentences.
   a They (to go) to live in Bahrain, because her dad has successfully found a new job.
   b I (to go) to live in France when I grow up, because I want (to be) a chef.
   c We (to go) study at university after school.
   d You (to go) to be the best soccer player in the world one day!
   e It (to go) to be difficult to achieve all he has set out to do, in such a short time.
   f She (to go) to be famous! She has such a beautiful voice.

LET'S TALK
Work in pairs. Imagine you are a famous sportsperson. Talk about the successes you have had and those that you are most proud of. Try and use some abstract nouns, like success, achievement, fame.

Compound nouns are made when you join two nouns together.

For example:

class + room = classroom

space + ship = spaceship

PRACTISE
How many compound nouns can you make by joining these words?

Swap lists with someone else. Who has the most words?

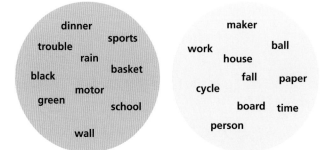

Gerunds are action nouns. They describe an activity. They are tricky, because they look like verbs. All gerunds end in -ing.

Here are some examples:

surfing	running	dancing	reading	sailing

You always use a gerund after these verbs: enjoy, like, dislike, avoid, keep, finish.

You also always use gerunds after certain prepositions, such as 'before' and 'after'.

The infinitive is the form of the verb with 'to' + the root verb. Here are some infinitives: to surf, to sail, to dance, to read. You can use an infinitive, or gerund, depending on the structure of a sentence.

Speaking my language

Try this

1   Quickly find all the gerunds in this paragraph.

> Surfing is my favourite sport. I don't like dancing, because I have no sense of rhythm. However, anything to do with the sea – surfing, sailing, fishing – you can count me in. Except diving – sorry I forgot to mention that. I don't like going underwater!

2   Now add gerunds or infinitives to these sentences so that they make sense. You can use the words in the box, or your own words.

   a   I enjoy _____, but my mother says we are not to do it after a meal.

   b   Let's get _____ on this project; we don't have much time.

   c   Before we go _____, shall we have dinner?

   d   I am training _____ a marathon next month.

   e   We plan to go _____ in the Swiss Alps after school.

   f   Most of my friends want _____ overseas when they finish school.

to dance	running	swimming	to hike	working
to work	to swim	hiking	to run	dancing

3   Prepare a short paragraph to say out loud about your favourite sport, or your goals for the future. Try and use these forms in your short talk:

   a   I love *running* ...

   b   I want to *run* ...

Reading

Surf's up!

1 Look up these words in your dictionary. Write down what they mean. Say them out loud and make sure to put the emphasis on the correct syllable.

segre*ga*tion	en*thu*siasm	com*mu*nity
volun*teer*	a*part*heid	ex*cite*ment

2 Learn to spell the words in the box.

3 You are going to read an interview with a surfer called Michael February. He comes from Cape Town in South Africa. In 2019, February was the first black African to make it to the World Tour.

Look out for these idiomatic expressions as you read. First discuss their meanings in your group. How would you use each expression in a sentence?

a Looking cool
b Into it
c A bunch
d Fired up
e Pretty epic

Michael February is helping to create a more diverse surfing future and looking good while he does it

There are few surfers in the world who look cool just going down the line, but Michael February is one of them.

Born in South Africa at the end of **apartheid**, February understands the history of **segregation** along his home coast in Cape Town, but he does not let the past weigh him down.

For February, it's all about the future, whether that means bettering his position on the World Tour (he is the first black African to qualify), volunteering with organisations to teach children to surf, or drawing new and dynamic lines on wave faces around the world.

When did you start surfing? I know you didn't take to it right away.

Yeah, it's funny because when I was 6 or 7 years old, my dad would try to take me surfing a bunch. But for whatever reason – maybe because it was my dad's thing and I didn't think it was cool – I was super fussy and didn't even stand up or anything. But later on I went with a friend of mine to a beach called Muizenberg for a surf lesson and stood up on my first wave and was immediately really into it. I think sometimes you maybe need to find something on your own for it to really stick.

Your dad has been a surfer in Cape Town since the time of apartheid. What was that like for him? Were there many black surfers in the area when he first started?

I don't think there were many, but he ended up finding other black surfers kind of by default because during apartheid you couldn't go to certain beaches if you were black. So all the black surfers would end up at the same spots. They ended up forming their own little surf community.

Though apartheid is over, do you feel that those tensions still exist in surfing in South Africa? Even in America, I've heard people of different backgrounds say that surfing can feel exclusively white at times.

I feel very fortunate because I was born around the same time that apartheid was ending, so by the time I started surfing, segregation at the beaches was long gone. In my experience, I never felt any kind of racial tension within the surfing community. Or maybe there was tension and I just didn't recognise it because I was so young.

What has your experience been like working with volunteer groups, getting kids into surfing and seeing the way they react to it?

It's been insane. In Cape Town, a lot of these kids live very close to the ocean, but they never went down to the water or experienced surfing before. But once these projects started, the kids realised that they had this playground right in front of them and they just love it. Their enthusiasm is crazy. One of the places we go in Cape Town with *Waves For Change* isn't a great wave, so the kids there don't see a lot of other surfers, and when you surf with them they get so fired up on any little turn that you do. You can honestly just do a cutback and all these kids on the beach will start cheering. It's pretty epic to see their excitement.

Now that you've made it onto the World Tour, does it feel significant to be the first black African in the top 34?

Yeah, I definitely do think about it. But I was very lucky to come from where I did, and to have a family that worked very hard so that I'd have all the opportunities and support in the world. I don't feel like it was more difficult for me to get to where I am because of the colour of my skin. But I definitely have a respect for the past and the struggles that happened before me. I feel like I'm part of a generation that's more free from that weight, and I like looking forward and looking at the positives. If a young kid in South Africa has never seen a person of colour surfing well or competing at a high level and they go, 'He looks like me. I can do that', then that's sick. But I'd hope that I'd be able to get people of all shapes and sizes and colours psyched on surfing.

Source: www.surfer.com

LET'S TALK

Discuss these questions in your group.
1   Do you think Michael February is a success? Explain why.
2   What was his dad's life like when he was young?
3   How was Michael's life different to his dad's?
4   What kind of volunteer work is Michael doing?
5   Would you like to meet Michael? Say why.

CHALLENGE YOURSELF

Can you work out what these phrases related to surfing mean?
● Going down the line.
● That dude totally snaked me!
● That dude got pitted!
● It's firing!

Writing

🔗 Running your own business

Read this comic about Ali and his successful business.

Writing your business plan

CHALLENGE YOURSELF

1 Work in groups. Using the information from the comic, write a step-by-step guide to how to plan a business. To do this, look at each frame of the comic and write down what Ali has done.

2 Exchange plans with another group. Help each other to fill in any missing information. Your teacher will help you with your final plan.

3 Use your step-by-step guide to plan a business in your group. Think about these questions:

a What are you going to make?

b How much will the materials cost?

c How much can you sell your items for?

d What equipment will you need to make and sell your product?

4 Finally, hold a market day at school. Each group can have its own stall from which to sell its product. Make big bold signs to advertise your product. Decide on the criteria for judging the most successful group, before the market day begins. (Who makes the most money? Who has the best plan? Who carries out their plan best? Who has the best product?)

Self check

After the market day, meet back in your group. Discuss your experience.

● How many products did you make? How many did you sell?
● Did you make a profit?
● What worked very well?
● What could you have done differently?
● Which group do you think was the most successful?
● How do they measure against the criteria you set before the market day?

What can you do?

● I can read, write and talk about what it means to be a success.
● I can read, write and talk about the future.
● I can read aloud and express my own opinion.
● I can listen to a podcast.
● I can write a basic business plan.

Now you have completed Unit 7, you may like to try the Unit 7 online knowledge test if you are using the Boost eBook.

8 The news

In this unit you will:

- listen to a radio programme about fake news
- talk about where we read the news
- read an article about how to spot fake news
- read reports that express different opinions
- role-play a news event
- use gerunds and reported speech
- write a news report in which you express an opinion.

Speaking and listening

How do you get news?

1 Most people hear or read at least some news every day. We have different **sources** of news, which means we get news in different ways or from different **media**. Work in groups and discuss where and how you get news every day. Here are some ideas:
- From friends (who?)
- From social media (which media?)
- From the television news (which programme?)
- On my phone or tablet (which website?)
- From the newspaper (which newspaper?)
- From different sources I see while travelling to school or work (which sources?).

2 Now talk about these questions.
   a Which of these is the best source of news? Why?
   b Which source gives you the most interesting news? Why?
   c Which source do you trust and believe? Why?
   d What is 'breaking news'?

Try this

Work in pairs. Read each of the headlines on the left.
1 Look up key words in your dictionary if you are not sure what they mean.
2 Discuss what you think this news is about.
3 Share your ideas with the class.

DID YOU KNOW?
Headlines are short phrases or parts of sentences. They are designed to attract attention and to be read quickly. Headlines help to sell newspapers and make people subscribe to electronic news services.

You are going to listen to four news headlines in Audio 8.1. For each headline, choose the correct sentence (a or b) below that gives the same information.

1 a A successful runner was unable to compete in the race because she began running before the starting pistol was fired.
   b The Olympic games will be stopped for five years.
2 a Climate change is slow.
   b The government is bringing in new laws about climate change.
3 a The local champions have broken the news.
   b In the latest news, we hear that a local team has won the championship league.
4 a You can learn to cook with famous people.
   b You can travel up to the stars and learn to cook.

HINT
Listen for the key nouns and verbs in the headlines.

Speaking and listening

Fake or fact?

We often see headlines about 'fake news' these days. But what is 'fake news'? Here is a definition:

> Fake news is news that is not true. It is information that *deliberately* tries to confuse or mislead us and make us believe the wrong information. Fake news appears in all media, from traditional newspapers, radio and television to social media.
>
> Fake news includes lies and **rumours**. The news can also **distort** information, which means to change it a little so that it means something else. This can make people upset and confused.

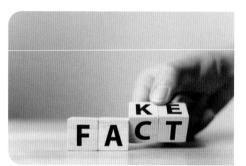 

Listen to Audio 8.2, which is a conversation about fake news. Listen again and choose the best phrase (a, b or c) to complete each sentence. Write the answers in your notebook.

1 The students are talking about the news that _____
   a the Health Ministry is to be banned.
   b public meetings are banned.
   c handshaking is to be banned.

2 Shaking hands with someone else can _____
   a spread germs.
   b be unfriendly.
   c be fake.

3 The students think the news is not fake because _____
   a it is silly.
   b it is part of their culture.
   c the news comes from good sources of information.

4 What other activities might also be banned, according to one student?
   a Hugging and kissing
   b Humming and skiing
   c Shaking and sleeping

Try this

Work in groups to play this game: 'Two Truths, One Lie'. Within your group, you will each prepare three statements about yourselves. Two statements must be true and one statement must be false (a lie). Pick things your classmates probably won't know about you – they can be as funny or as silly as you like. Just make sure it's not obvious which are true and which is false. Each member of the group will take their turn to read their statements to the class. The class has to work out which statements are true and which are false by asking you questions. Work out a scoring system for this game before you play – the winning group will be the one that had the most false statements picked as truths by the class.

HINT

Remember not to let on to the rest of the class which of your statements is true and which a lie. Try not to laugh!

LET'S TALK

Look at the message on the screen in the photograph below. Think about what you know about 'fake news'.
1 What do you think this message means?
2 What type of media does the message refer to? How do you know this?

DID YOU KNOW?

Some social media services close fake accounts that spread false or untrue information.

Fake accounts are not your friends.

Facebook is changing so you see more from your friends, and less of the stuff that gets in the way.

James Anderson posted a photo
Tuesday at 5.04 PM

Seun Shobande and 81 others   7 Comments

Like   Comment   Share

Use of English

Gerunds

The following two sentences have the same meaning, but one is written with an infinitive and the other with a gerund. Can you say which is which?

- I love to read the news every morning.
- I love reading the news every morning.

A gerund can be the *subject* of a sentence.

For example:

Cooking is my passion!

In this sentence the gerund is before the verb.

A gerund can be the *object* of a sentence.

For example:

I have stopped reading the news, because I don't believe it anymore!

In this sentence the gerund is after the verb in the main clause.

PRACTISE

1 Read these sentences and identify the gerunds. Are the gerunds the subject or object of each sentence? Write your answers in your notebook.
   a Handshaking spreads germs.
   b Washing our hands is important.
   c Do people enjoy watching the news on television?
   d Stopping climate change is not going to be easy.
   e The tennis player admitted fixing the match.
   f Thousands of people enjoyed the dancing last night.

2 Now listen to these sentences in Audio 8.3. Listen to the word stress in the gerunds. What do you notice? Is the -ing sound stressed or not stressed?

3 Work in pairs. Read each sentence aloud to your partner.

Try this

Write these sentences in your notebook, using the correct gerund form in each sentence.
1 (Kiss) in public will not be allowed in public places.
2 (Run) is good for your health, says a health expert.
3 I hate (watch) the news because it's always bad news.
4 Fake news can cause panic (buy) if people believe there will be a shortage of goods.
5 My grandmother remembers (listen) to the radio only for the news.
6 (Travel) can be dangerous, so read factual information about your trip before you leave.

After some verbs we can use an infinitive or a gerund. For example:

I love reading

I love to read.

But not all verbs are like this. The following verbs are always followed by a gerund:

✓ I <u>enjoy</u> reading.

✓ <u>Keep</u> smiling, even when things are difficult.

✓ Would you <u>mind</u> passing me the newspaper?

✓ Have you <u>finished</u> reading all the news?

✓ <u>Stop</u> watching the news on that fake service.

We do not say:

✗ I enjoy to read.

✗ Keep to smile, even when things are difficult.

✗ Would you mind to pass me the newspaper?

✗ Have you finished to read all the news?

✗ Stop to watch the news on that fake service.

Try this

Work in pairs and complete the conversation. Make gerunds with the words in the box.

run	hug	teach	bump	be	smile	dance	play	enjoy

Alya: Have you heard the news? _____ is banned!

Mika: That's fake news! Why would they do that?

Alya: They say _____ elbows is better.

Mika: Oh? So you don't catch germs, I suppose.

Alya: Yes. Oh well. At least we can try and keep _____!

Mika: Yes. _____ the good things that we have is a good idea.

Alya: Right. I'm finished _____ miserable. Can we go _____?

Mika: Would you mind _____ me how to dance? I'm not very good at it!

Alya: How about _____ some football!

Mika: Now you are talking!

Alya: Hey stop _____ so fast! I can't keep up.

CHALLENGE YOURSELF

Rewrite these sentences so that each sentence has a gerund.

1 My mother loves to watch the news on television.

2 To wash your hands with soap and water or a sanitiser is very important.

3 It is a bit silly to believe everything you read.

4 It is never a good idea to cheat in sport.

Reading

Texts that inform us

Some texts inform us because they give us factual information. For example, a magazine or newspaper article may tell us how many people visited a tourist destination in one year. This means that someone counted these visits, or that this is based on the number of tickets that were sold.

Texts can also inform us by giving us instructions, warnings and advice. For example, how to wash your hands properly to get rid of germs or directions on how to leave a building in the event of a fire.

1 Before you read:
  a Look at the text below quickly and tell a partner what you think you will learn from it.
  b Discuss what the term 'to **fact-check**' means.
  c Does this writer have an opinion about fact-checking? What is that opinion? Write down your answer and check it after you have read the text.
2 Read the article silently by yourself.

Fact-checking is important

As you know, there is a lot of fake news out there. Some people call this '**disinformation**' or '**misinformation**'. So how do you know what is fake and what is true? It would be so handy if we could click a 'fact-check' button on our phones or laptops, but unfortunately we cannot do that yet. But we can and *must* all do some fact-checking before we believe all the news we hear. We check information about products before we buy them, so we should also check the news.

How to fact-check news

Ask yourself these questions about the news you are reading:
1 The source of the news:
  ● Why do I trust the source?
  ● Who sent it to me?
  ● Is it just a rumour or can I check the 'facts' on another source?
2 The quality of the news:
  ● Are there spelling and grammar mistakes?
  ● Does it seem to be incomplete?
  ● Are there lots of different images and not much information?
  ● Is it full of words which seem to exaggerate things or make them seem worse?
  ● Is it trying to persuade or influence me to believe something (that may not be true)?
  ● Is the news very pro- (for) or anti- (against) some idea or event?
3 The pictures or photographs:
  ● Are these real photographs or have they been **manipulated** in some way?
  ● Do the pictures relate to this news event (or are they from another event)?

Who would you believe about health matters? The national or public health ministry or service which is run by your government, or a friend on Twitter?

Vocabulary and spelling

1 Match the words and their meanings.

Something that many people are talking about and repeating, but may not be true	distort
To change something so that its sound, shape or meaning is not accurate or clear	**lie**
To persuade people to believe or do something that might not be true or right	rumour
Something that is not true	manipulate

2 Look at the meanings of the prefixes in the box below. Use the information to work out the meanings of these words:
   a Disinformation   c Pro-democracy
   b Misinformation   d Anti-democracy

Prefix	Meaning	Example
dis	not, the opposite of	disagree
mis	wrong, bad	misbehave
pro-	supporting, in favour of	pro-government
anti-	against, not supporting	anti-smoking

 3 Learn to spell the words in the box below. Work with a partner. Look carefully at each word first and discuss why the word has or does not have a double consonant. Then copy, cover and write the words again.

handshaking	fact-checking	bumping	breaking
running	reading	smiling	hugging

4 Now write each word in the infinitive form. Which letters may you need to add or drop? For example:

handshaking = handshake

Try this

CHALLENGE YOURSELF

Find a short article in a news service that you use often. Try fact-checking it. Then rewrite the article so that it provides only fact-checked information.

1 Work in pairs. Find an example of a short piece of current news. The news may be true or it may be fake. You can look in any media that you read regularly.
   ● Write the news on a sheet of paper.
   ● Show it to the class.
   ● State the source of the news.

2 Ask the rest of the class to vote on whether they think the news is fake or true. Then tell them the correct answer and explain why the news is true or false.

Use of English

Reporting what others say

A famous chef once said that cooking was her passion. Her actual words were, 'Cooking is my passion'. The first sentence is in reported speech and the second sentence is in direct speech.

Try this

Work with a partner. Read this section of a news report. Work out what words the mayor actually used. Discuss this with another pair until you agree. Write out the passage in your notebook, changing the text to use direct speech.

> The mayor said that that the organisers had no choice about **cancelling** the music festival. It was all due to the weather forecasts for the weekend. Huge storms and the possibility of flooding were forecast. He said public safety was his biggest **concern**. He asked for our understanding but said that he could not change the weather.

Do you remember?

Reported speech: We use reported speech to say what someone said.

For example:

> The man said that the news was fake. (Statement)
>
> My teacher says we must not believe everything we read. (Command)

Direct speech: We use this in stories and to quote the actual words that someone spoke. Direct speech is always inside speech marks (' and ').

PRACTISE

1   Write the following statements in reported speech.
a   'I will watch the news on television this evening,' said my father.
b   'You must fact-check what you read,' said Anya.
c   'Not all news is fake news,' the reporter said.
d   'I read two news reports every day so that I get two opinions,' said Mr Lee.

2   Write the following commands in reported speech.
a   'Always fact-check the news,' my mother advised.
b   'Please look at me,' the news photographer said.
c   'Do not read all that fake news!' the man shouted.
d   'You must not manipulate the facts!' the reporter said.

HINT

When you need to change direct speech to reported speech, do the following:
- Look at the word order.
- Look at the verb tenses.
- Look at the pronouns.
- Look at words that express time.
- Notice how the word 'if' is used.

Try this

Work in pairs. Study the following questions and requests carefully. How do the sentences change in reported speech? Prepare your sentences and then report back to the class.

1   'Can you teach me how to dance?' Mika asked Alya.
Mika asked Alya if she could teach him how to dance.

2   'Have you heard the news?' Alya asked Mika.
Alya asked Mika if he had heard the news.

HINT

Remember to use 'if' in your reported questions and requests.

PRACTISE

1   Read the following questions aloud with a partner. Then discuss how to write them in reported speech.
a   'Do you know what the time is?' Pete asked me.
b   'Are those photographs real?' the reporter asked the photographer.
c   'Is this fake news, Dad?' Mara asked.
d   'Do you trust the source of this news?' our teacher asked us.
e   'Is that a rumour or is it true?' my friend asked me.
f   'Can I check these facts on the internet?' Kara asked her teacher.

2   Now write the following requests in reported speech in your notebook.
a   'Can we go (dance)?' Alya asked.
b   'Can you help me tomorrow?' Jo asked Ben.
c   'May I read that newspaper?' the woman on the train asked me.
d   'May my son sit here?' the man on the train asked me.

CHALLENGE YOURSELF

Work in small groups of three to four students. Each person asks a question about fake news, or another topic suggested by your teacher. The next person in the group reports the question. Take turns until everyone has asked a question. The group can try to answer each question quickly. For example:

Sanjay: Is the news about our football team fake?

Milo: Sanjay asked if the news about their football team was fake.

Reading

Read news reports that express opinions

1 Work in groups. Read these reported statements. Which ones do you think are based on fact and which are opinions? How do you know?
   a The referee said that she thought it was a fair match.
   b The report said that the blue team won by three goals to two.
   c The mayor said in her view the event should be cancelled.
   d The mayor said that the event was cancelled.

Vocabulary

2 Read the following two reports carefully. The reports are about the same event.

Text A

Heartbreak as music festival is cancelled

<u>Heart-breaking</u> news! The much-loved New Light Music Festival has been <u>cancelled</u> at the last minute. No more festival this weekend. This has been done for our own safety – apparently! And the organisers and city management team are blaming it all on the weather. What a poor excuse!

In his announcement on social media last night, the mayor said that the organisers had no choice. It was all due to the weather forecasts for the weekend, which predicted thunderstorms and gale-force winds. He said public safety was his biggest concern. He asked for our understanding but said that he could not change the weather.

When asked if the festival would be <u>postponed</u> to a later date, the mayor said that he wasn't sure. He was very <u>vague</u> about this. Will it happen or not? No one seems to know! He didn't announce any definite plans.

The mayor and his team also seem to have forgotten the <u>knock-on effects</u> of the cancellation! Preparing for the festival has taken up a lot of time and money. Traders have already prepared food which they hoped to sell during the festival. Equipment has been hired and performers have been booked.

The mayor also failed to mention that the bad weather was also forecast to improve on Sunday morning and not last the whole weekend. This leads me to believe that perhaps there is another reason behind this sudden cancellation. We can't always blame the weather!

Text B

Music festival cancelled

The New Light Music Festival has been cancelled due to severe weather warnings for the coming weekend. The forecasts are for thunderstorms, heavy rain and strong winds. Thousands of ticket holders have expressed their disappointment at the decision.

Keeping the festival goers in mind, the mayor said that the event had been cancelled in the interests of public safety. He said that the festival might be postponed until a later date. He promised that he and his team would discuss this carefully. Apologising for the cancellation, the mayor asked for understanding.

 3 Find the words in the box in the texts. They are underlined. Work in pairs and discuss what each word or expression means. Look for clues in the sentence or in the paragraph in which the word occurs.

heart-breaking	**vague**	heavy rain
cancelled	knock-on effects	understanding
postponed	**severe**	

4 Choose five of the words from the list above and make your own sentences with them.

5 Look at Text A. Does this writer express an opinion about the event? Choose **two** of the statements below to support your answer.
   a The festival should not have been cancelled.
   b He agrees that the mayor was correct to cancel the festival.
   c He thinks that the weather was used as an excuse to cancel the festival.
   d He thinks it is fine to have the festival at a different time.

6 Look at Text B. Does this writer express an opinion? Choose **two** statements to support your answer.
   a The writer thinks it is the correct decision.
   b The writer thinks that the mayor and his team will carefully consider having the festival on another day.
   c The writer is very angry with the mayor and his team.
   d The writer does not believe the excuse that the weather is to blame for the cancellation.

7 What do you think? Should the festival have been cancelled? Write a short paragraph. State your opinion clearly and then give two reasons to support your answer, based on what you have read.

Speaking and listening

Listening to and giving opinions

1 You are going to give your group a short news report in which you state the facts about an event and give your opinion about it. Before you do this, listen to the way a reporter states facts and opinions about an event in Audio 8.4.

   a Make notes of any words or phrases that state facts.

   b Make notes about statements that are vague (i.e. not facts).

   c Make notes of words the reporter uses to state her opinion.

2 Now prepare for your discussion and work with your group.

   a Read the day's news (or news that is quite recent). Use your phone or the internet or a newspaper.

   b Find two articles about the same event.

   c Make notes on three facts about the event.

   d Prepare a very short news report to give to your group. Your report must describe the event. To do this, state at least three facts. End the report by stating your own opinion about the event.

3 Finally, take turns to present your short reports to the rest of the group.

   a Listen carefully to what others in the group have to say. As you listen, write down one question that you would like to ask each person.

   b Take turns to ask each speaker a few questions.

> **HINT**
> Make notes in any way that will help you. Some people like to write key words. Others prefer to write down whole sentences in large print!

> **HINT**
> It doesn't matter if you make a few mistakes. Just try to speak clearly.

PRACTISE

▲ Avocadoes

1 Look at the photograph.
- Do you know this fruit?
- What does it taste like?
- Do you like it?
- Do you eat it?

2 Listen to the report about a fashionable health food in Audio 8.5. Then complete these sentences in your notebook.

I have eaten _____ pears since I was a _____ child. We grew them _____ the farm where I _____. For us they were just _____ – like apples or oranges. _____ when we lived in central _____, we bought avocadoes along the _____ of the road. They were _____ and abundant.

I live in a _____ city now and things have _____. Avocadoes are fashionable! And that _____ they are also expensive!

3 When you have completed the sentences, listen to the report and check your own work.

HINT

Don't forget to:
- read your completed sentences carefully to see if they make sense
- use a pencil to circle or underline words that do not make sense
- listen again carefully for the words you are not sure about.

Writing

Write a news report with an opinion

1 You have read two news reports about a cancelled music festival. Read Text A on page 132 again.

a Write down three facts from the report.

b Write down three sentences in which the writer expresses an opinion. Keep these notes as they will help you when you write your own report.

2 Read the facts in the box below about an argument over pasta that occurred in Australia. It is true. You may even have seen something like this on a YouTube clip. It occurred during a recent world-wide health scare.

A supermarket struggle over pasta

- The argument took place in Sydney, Australia.
- Two women were in a supermarket.
- They both wanted to stock up on pasta.
- They were afraid there would be a shortage of pasta.
- The first woman grabbed ten packets of pasta on the shelf.
- The second woman only got one packet.
- She shouted, 'That's not fair! Give me five of those packets.'
- The other woman shouted, 'No, I won't. I got here first.'
- The woman tried to grab the packets. They fell and the packets broke.
- There was pasta all over the floor.

HINT

- Give your reader the main facts in the first paragraph. Give information that answers these questions: Who? What? Where? How? Without this information the reader will not be able to understand the report.
- Use exclamation marks with your opinions to show how you feel. For example: What a silly argument! Some people don't think before they act!

Try this

Now plan, draft, edit and write a news report about this event. Your article should have three or four paragraphs (about 150 words). Use the facts given above. State your opinion about the event quite clearly and give reasons to support this.

Remember that you can change the way the sentences are written in the list of facts above.

For example:

The woman tried to grab the packets = The woman tried grabbing the packets from the other.

(Use a gerund and add a phrase.)

HINT

- Draft your article and give it to a friend to read. Let your friend suggest how you can improve it. For example, did you give your reader all the important information in the first paragraph?
- Remember to check your spelling!

CHALLENGE YOURSELF

Write an article in which you express a different opinion about the same event. For example, you could express sympathy or support for either of the two women who argued over pasta in Australia.

Self check

- Did you use reported speech to report what the people said to each other? Read the notes on pages 130–31 again if necessary.
- Did you use at least two gerunds in your report to make your writing more interesting?

What can you do?

Read and review what you can do.
- I can listen to a radio programme about fake news.
- I can talk about where we read the news.
- I can read an article about how to spot fake news.
- I can read reports that express different opinions.
- I can role-play a news event.
- I can use gerunds and reported speech.
- I can write a news report in which I express an opinion.

 Now you have completed Unit 8, you may like to try the Unit 8 online knowledge test if you are using the Boost eBook.

9 Far, far away

In this unit you will:

- listen to a programme about where movies are filmed
- talk about visiting and living in remote places
- listen to a podcast about how to survive in a **remote** place
- read about a film location
- read about the challenges of living in remote places
- write a story about living in a remote place
- use a range of different adjectives and quantifiers
- use relative clauses.

▲ A remote island in Raja Ampat, Indonesia

▲ A village in the mountains around Jajarkot, Nepal

▲ Inside a tent in the Agafay desert, Morocco

▲ In the Phang Nga National Park, Koh Yao Yai, Thailand

Speaking and listening

 Remote places

1 A 'remote' place is a place that is far away from where most people live. Work in groups and discuss these questions. Share your ideas with the class.

   a Do you live in a place that is far away from cities and public transport? If you do, where is the nearest town or bus?

   b Have you ever travelled to a place where very few people live? How did you get there? How long did it take?

2 Work in pairs. Read the captions under the photographs on page 138. Talk about:

- why each place is remote
- which place you would like to visit
- why you would like to visit one of the places
- what you would do in that place.

> **HINT**
>
> Try to express your ideas, even if you are not sure how to say something or if you make mistakes. Others will understand you and they can ask questions if they don't!

Try this

 Listen to the podcast extracts in Audio 9.1. The notes below were written by people who had visited the places in the photographs on page 138. Read these while you listen to the podcasts. Then match each of them to one of the photographs.

> **CHALLENGE YOURSELF**
>
> Imagine that you had visited one of the remote places in the photographs. Write two sentences to describe what you did and enjoyed at the place.

Where would you go? What would you do?

1 Went diving in the sea. There is so much to see here! Loads of beautiful fish, underwater plants, shells.

2 The forest was eerie and so quiet. There were no other people, but plenty of birds and insect noises. At times it was a little scary being alone, but at the same time it was beautiful too.

3 On our climb up into the mountains, we came across this village. The view from here was stunning – can see the valleys and mountains all around. Wondered what it would be like to live here though? It's so high up!

4 The desert is so hot but then you step into one of these beautiful tents, with everything that you need. And they can be packed up and moved along to another place quite easily too.

 PRACTISE

Work in pairs. Listen to the podcasts again carefully. Which words are stressed in each sentence? How do the voices change when there are exclamation marks or question marks? Take turns to read the texts to your partner using the same intonation.

Speaking and listening

On location

Film makers sometimes use remote places for filming. For example, the TV series *I'm a Celebrity … Get Me Out of Here!* was filmed in national parks in Australia. The films based on the *Lord of the Rings* books were filmed in the mountains and forests of New Zealand. Other film locations are cities or on **film sets** that have been specially built for the film. Some films are also made inside, in **studios**.

1 Before you listen to the podcast in Audio 9.2, look at the photographs and read the captions.

2 Now listen to Audio 9.2 and match each podcast to a photograph.

▲ A film crew using a beach as a location

▲ On set on the streets of Berlin in Germany

◀ This film set is in Suncheon, South Korea. This town was specially built for filming. Tourists come to visit the set too

▲ Can you guess which films were made here on the island of Oahu in Hawaii?

▲ Old castles are used to make films set in medieval times

DID YOU KNOW?

People often talk about 'shooting' a film. For example:

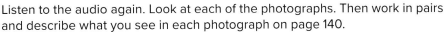

The film was shot in India.

We're shooting in London today.

PRACTISE

Listen to the audio again. Look at each of the photographs. Then work in pairs and describe what you see in each photograph on page 140.
- Where is this?
- What are people doing?
- What type of film is made in this location?

Try this

Work in pairs. Talk about your favourite films or TV series. Choose two of these and find out where the film or series was made. Try to find a photograph of the location as well.

Then do a brief presentation to the class about the films you have chosen. Your presentation should not be longer than one minute. You can use pictures to support what you are saying.

HINT

There are several websites on the internet that can help you to find out about film locations. They will also give you additional information about films, such as who the actors are.

DID YOU KNOW?

A film crew is a group of people who work together to make a film. The crew consists of directors, sound and lighting engineers, caterers, film photographers, directors, make-up artists, people who look after costumes and many more. A film crew for a TV film series could be between 150 and 500 people!

LET'S TALK

Work in groups. Talk about what happens when a film crew moves into an area to make a film.
- How does this affect the people and animals that live there?
- How does this affect the natural environment?
- Think about positive and negative effects.

Use of English

Adjectives

> ### Do you remember?
>
> Adjectives are very useful in descriptions because they tell us more about nouns and allow us to make comparisons.
>
> For example:
>
> > This is a <u>remote</u> place in Australia.
> >
> > That is the <u>most beautiful</u> place I have ever visited.
> >
> > It was an <u>exciting</u> film. I was not <u>bored</u> for the whole two hours!

Can you identify the adjectives in the following sentences?

1 I'm so excited – we're going to New Zealand where they filmed *The Lord of the Rings*!
2 The natural surroundings make up a beautiful set.
3 Castles are also popular locations.
4 The forest was eerie and quiet.
5 The view from here was stunning.

Compound adjectives

Some adjectives consist of two words. We call these compound adjectives. We usually write these adjectives with a hyphen. Study the following examples.

- We took a <u>five-hour</u> tour of the film set.
- This travel guide is <u>second-hand</u>, but it is still useful.
- Do you live in an <u>English-speaking</u> country?
- This is a <u>brand-new</u> film set.

> **PRACTISE**
>
> Work in pairs.
>
> 1 Use one word from each column to make compound adjectives that will fit into the sentences below. You should be able to make at least eight words.
>
> | seven easy one well good second   250 | day hour behaved looking known   hand page going |
> |---|---|
>
> a We are going on a _____ -_____ trip to South Korea next month.
> b My friend is such an _____-_____ person. I feel relaxed when I am with her.
> c We had a quick _____-_____ tour around the film studio.

➡

    d I have a _____-_____ book to read before I leave on my trip.
    e The actor who plays the main role in the film is so _____-_____!
    f All the people on the tour bus were _____-_____. No one caused any trouble.

2 See if you can find the words you have made in your dictionary. Check the meanings.

Try this

Using a compound adjective instead of a long phrase can improve your style of writing. Look at these examples:

A <u>walk of ten minutes</u> along the beach is refreshing.

A <u>ten-minute walk</u> along the beach is refreshing.

I <u>usually use my left</u> hand to do things but I play tennis with my racquet in my right hand.

I am usually <u>left-handed</u> but I play tennis with my racquet in my right hand.

Work in pairs and replace the underlined words in these sentences with compound adjectives. You will have to change the word order in the sentences as well.

1 We went on a trip that lasted two weeks.
2 Do you see that woman? She is an actor whom many people know.
3 Are you someone who uses their right hand for most things?

We can form adjectives with the suffixes -ing and -ed. For example:

I am so <u>excited</u> about the trip.

It was a very <u>exciting</u> trip.

The tour of the film studio was <u>boring</u>.

I was <u>bored</u> during the tour of the film studio.

The problem is that the adjectives do not have exactly the same meaning.

1 Which adjectives in the sentences above describe how a person feels?
2 Which adjectives describe a noun that causes you to have a feeling?

PRACTISE

Choose the correct word to complete each sentence in your notebook.

1 It was such a (tired/tiring) day. I need to sleep.
2 The film director is very (worrying/worried) because we are filming on the beach and a storm is coming.
3 The film crew is very (pleased/pleasing) with the new film set they have built.
4 That is such an (amusing/amused) film! You should see it.
5 I was quite (disturbed/disturbing) by that film. It was scary.

HINT

Look at the nouns in the underlined phrases. You can also look up the noun in your dictionary and you will find compound adjectives with that noun. Choose the best one if there is more than one.

CHALLENGE YOURSELF

Work in small groups and talk about your favourite films. Use the following words and phrases to compare the films.

lots of

as much as

not as much as

more exciting than

less entertaining than

Reading

Travel blogs

Some people like to travel to remote places and they post blogs about their travels. Before you read these have a quick look at the blogs. Which one looks the most interesting to you?

The land of upside-down trees and lemurs …

Madagascar, in the Indian Ocean, is such a special place in so many ways. It's an island off the east coast Africa where you can see many different animals. I just love the lemurs. They're the cute little creatures that have long stripy tails. You can see them at the national parks like Andasibe and Ranomafana.

And then you have to take a drive out into the country to see the baobab trees. Some people call them 'upside down' trees because they look as if their roots are up in the air instead of in the ground. Some of these ancient trees are hundreds of years old. They have seen so much!

And the Malagasy people are super-friendly …

▲ Lemurs

▲ An avenue of baobab trees in Madagascar

Waterfalls that sound like thunder

Dynjandi waterfall is – breathtaking! It is one of the biggest waterfalls in Iceland. It's a cold place and it's far away but it is also very special. The Dybjandi waterfall is actually not just one waterfall – there are several waterfalls. But the one in the photograph is the one that people like to visit. When you stand in front of it you can feel the power of the water … the word dynjandi means 'like thunder' and yes, it is also quite noisy! You can take a 15-minute walk up along the side of the waterfall too. You'll get a bit wet, but it's really worth the effort to see such a beautiful sight.

▲ Dynjandi, the big waterfall in Iceland

Far, far away in time and place

If you like old buildings, the Veerabhadra temple in Lepakshi, India, is a 'must-see'. It is an important national monument in the state of Andhra Pradesh in India, which is in the south-eastern part of the country. The temple was built in 1530, which is almost five hundred years ago! Every surface is carved or painted. To get there, it's a three-hour journey north of Bangalore in India. You travel for about 140 km, through small villages.

▲ Veerabhadra Temple, Lepakshi, India

Vocabulary and spelling

HINT

Synonyms are words that have similar, but perhaps not exactly the same meaning.

1 Find synonyms for these words in the blogs above.
a Pretty, attractive, usually small too
b An animal
c Many
d Strength
e (Patterns or pictures) cut out of wood or stone
f The outside part of something

HINT

The adjectives in the sentences in question 2 are compound adjectives. What does each adjective mean?

2 Work in pairs and discuss what the underlined words mean.
a It is <u>breath-taking</u>.
b The people are <u>super-friendly</u>.
c It is in the <u>south-eastern</u> part of the country.
d It is a <u>15-minute</u> walk up to the top of the waterfall.

3 Read these sentences. The underlined words in each sentence are incorrectly spelled. Find the correct spelling in the blogs above and then practise writing each word correctly.
a Have you seen the <u>waterfal</u>? It is <u>beautifull.</u>
b I think I would like to live alone on an <u>iland</u> in the middle of the <u>oshun</u>.
c My parents love to visit <u>nasional</u> monuments. I prefer to admire <u>animels</u>.
d Baobabs are often <u>anshient</u> trees. Many are <u>hundrets</u> of years old.

LET'S TALK

Work in groups. Think about the blogs you read above and discuss these questions.
1 Would you like to visit any of these places? Why? Why not?
2 Would you like to live in any of these places? Why? Why not?
3 Would any of these places make a good film set? For what type of film?

Share your ideas informally with the rest of the class.

Use of English

Describing quantities

Do you remember?

Quantifiers are words that describe quantities. They tell us *how many* or *how much* there is of something.

Can you identify the quantifiers in this paragraph?

> There is so much to see under the sea here! There are loads of beautiful fish, underwater plants and shells. There are no people, but plenty of fish. All of the fish are beautiful. I saw lots of grey ones and many others with bright colours and stripes. Some fish have long fins and tails.

How do we use few and most? Put the quantifier before the noun. Do you understand the difference between a few and few? For example:

A few people at my school have been to this place.

Few people at my school have been to this place.

Most people at my school have visited this place.

How do we use both and all? We do not use articles with these quantifiers. You can use 'of' after 'both' and 'all' but you do not have to do this. For example:

Both of/Both my grandparents have visited Madagascar.

All of/All my friends enjoy going on trips.

PRACTISE

Work with a partner and read these sentences aloud, choosing the correct words as you read.

1 There are (loads of/loads) wonderful places to visit in India.

2 There are (no/none) shops on the island, so take (some/the some) food with you.

3 I have seen (a few/the few) films that were filmed in Malta. We are going there in (a few/few) days.

4 We are visiting Malaysia next year because (all of/the all) my cousins live there.

5 (The both/Both) of the photographs show what the waterfall looks like.

Relative clauses

Do you remember?

Relative clauses are clauses that begin with relative pronouns such as 'who', 'that' or 'which'. These pronouns link the clauses. We use 'who' to refer to people.

Find the relative clauses in these sentences.
1   This is the woman who made that wonderful film.
2   My grandfather, who is 67, has never travelled to the USA.
3   Other film locations are cities or on sets that have been specially built for the film.
4   We walked past the street which is being used as a film set.

HINT
Remember that a clause must have its own verb.

Relative pronouns such as 'whom', 'whose', 'where' and 'why' can also be used to connect clauses. For example:

This is the actor *whose* mother was also a famous actor.

I saw the family *whom** I had met last year.

This is the reason *why* they chose this location for the film!

Do you know *where* Uganda is?

**whom* is quite formal. Many people would use 'who' or 'that' in this sentence.

Try this

Choose the best relative pronoun to complete each sentence.
1   We will visit a castle (who/which) has been used as a film set.
2   Please tell me (why/which) you went to that remote place.
3   This is the bridge (that/whom) connects the two towns.
4   I showed my friends a photograph (that/who) I had taken of the waterfall.
5   Mr Lee, (that/who) lives in Hong Kong, is a friend of my dad's.
6   Please show me on a map (where/why) you went last week.

Reading

Remote living

Before you read this magazine article, which expresses someone's account and opinions about living in a remote place, stop and read the following list. Which of these things are things that you *need* to survive on a remote place?

shelter	a house	gas	bottled water	a horse	clothes
a tent	electricity	food	a car	a book to read	**solar-powered** lights

Can you add anything to the list of needs?

Now read the magazine article. The writer wrote this story about her feelings and experiences when she and her family went to live in a remote place. As you read, try to understand the writer's opinion about the time she spent in this remote place.

Time on an island, away from it all

▲ The house we stayed in on the Isle of Skye

Last year our family moved away from the city. I suppose you are wondering why we went? I have asked myself that question many times. The official reason was that my mum was writing a book, and she needed peace and quiet. Well, maybe she did ... I think we all did.

Anyway, we moved out to this cottage on the Isle of Skye in Scotland, which is connected to the mainland by a bridge. It was a two-day trip to get there. When we arrived in Inverness we took a train. Then we took a bus which drove us across the Skye Bridge to the island.

We took absolutely everything that we thought we might need with us. We had food and solar-powered lamps and loads of warm clothes. We took books, tablets, movies and games which were supposed to keep us entertained. Honestly, I'm not sure why we took so much stuff!

At first it was fun. We went for long walks to explore the area. I now understand what a '**rugged landscape**' means. There are lots of mountains and rocks and nothing is flat! We became quite fit. We had fun playing games that my parents used to play before the days of electronic games. We enjoyed the fresh air and looked at the stars at night. I learned to identify many stars that I have never even heard of before. I now know where the Milky Way is, for example. It's easy to see the stars here because there is no pollution and hardly any lights. I also learned how to make a fire, which I had never done before. We visited an old castle which had been used as a film set too!

But after a while we realised that there were challenges as well. I found it hard not to be in constant contact with my friends. I missed them and I couldn't even chat on social media every day because the Wi-Fi connection wasn't very good. I started to fight with my brother because he is so noisy. I think he was missing his friends too.

We stayed there for two months. Now that we are back home, I think it was a good experience. I learned a lot about the world around me and I also learned how to entertain myself. But I don't think I could live in a place like that all the time!

Vocabulary

Choose the word that best describes each word.

1 Rugged
   a Bumpy
   b Flat
2 Isle
   a Mainland
   b Island
3 To miss (someone)
   a Not to know where someone has gone
   b To feel sad because you don't see or talk to someone
4 Experience
   a Something that you do all the time
   b Something that has happened to you

Write your answers to these questions in your notebook.

5 Where did the author go with her family?
6 How did they get to this place?
7 What is the Milky Way?
   a A group of stars in the sky
   b The place where you go to buy milk
   c A place in Scotland
   d A star
8 What did the author think about all the things they took with them to the island?
   a She thought it was a bit silly.
   b She thought that they had taken too much.
   c She thought all the things were not really necessary.
   d All of these answers are true.
9 How did the author feel about the place when she first arrived?
   a She was afraid.
   b She enjoyed herself.
   c She hated the place.
   d She wanted to leave.
10 Explain how the author felt after the family had spent some time on the island. For example, did her opinion change?
11 Find two challenges and two benefits the author experienced when living on the island.
12 What do you think? Would you like to spend time in a place like this? Give two reasons for your answer.

> **CHALLENGE YOURSELF**
>
> Write a description of the place where the author of this magazine article stayed. Look at the photograph on page 148 carefully first.

Speaking and listening

Negotiating

1 Listen to Audio 9.3, which is a discussion some students are having about a school trip. Listen to the way in which they **negotiate** with each other until they agree on what to do. Listen to the tone of voice they use as they negotiate with each other.

2 Now read the text you listened to below and make a note of useful words that Ken, Adi, Asrif and Sarah used to negotiate in the discussion.

A school trip

Ken: Hi everyone. As you know, we need to discuss our trip next year. The school has said that we should give them ideas about where we want to go next year.

Adi: Great. We're *not* going to that place on the lake again. It's too far and it's full of *mosquitoes* – and there's *no Wi-Fi!*

Asrif: Maybe. But that is the point, isn't it? We are supposed to do something we *don't* usually do?

Sarah: Yes, I think so, but last year I felt as if I was on one of those 'survivor' programmes you see on TV. It was all too tough and uncomfortable.

Ken: OK, you have a point. So we want to go to a place that is not *too* uncomfortable …

Adi: … and that has *proper* beds, *Wi-Fi* …

Asrif: *Wait a minute*! We have those at home. Surely we want a place that is *different*?

Sarah: Well, maybe … yes. Perhaps a place that is *not* too far away and *not* too uncomfortable.

Ken: OK. A **compromise** then. Now let's make some suggestions.

DID YOU KNOW?

'To compromise' means to reach an agreement in which each of you get part of what you would like, but not everything. When we do things in groups, we usually have to compromise because people have different needs or ideas.

PRACTISE

Work in groups of five. Your school has proposed a school trip to a high mountain area next year. The school has asked for your input and suggestions. Each group is going to debate the trip. To prepare for the debate, each person in the group has to prepare some notes.

Step 1: Look at the diagram and choose the topic that you would like to talk about.

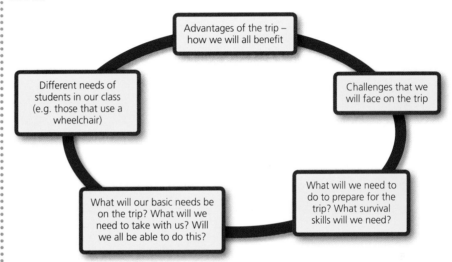

Step 2: Work alone and prepare your notes.

Step 3: Take turns to make your short presentations to your group.

Step 4: Now discuss the ideas that you have heard. You will have to reach a compromise, which means you will have to agree on some things.

Step 5: Once you have agreed on what your group thinks, present your group's views to the rest of the class. Then debate the topic as a class until you reach a compromise.

Writing

Magazine article

You have read an article about someone's feelings and experiences of living in a remote place. You may have a similar experience or you may not. So let's imagine that we are going to live in a remote place.

 Start by looking at the following photographs with a partner. Read the captions. Look up the places on a map and then try to describe each place.

- What challenges would you face if you went to live there?
- What would the advantages (positive things) be?

▲ Ban Ruam, a village up in the mountains in northern Thailand

▲ A Uros house on an artificial, floating island in southern Peru

▲ Traditional homes of the Turkana people in Kenya, Africa

Try this

Now plan, draft, edit and write a magazine article about your experiences in a remote place. Your article should have three or four paragraphs (about 150 words). State your opinion about the experience quite clearly and give reasons. You could also describe how you felt at first and how your feelings changed.

Once you have written a draft of your article, read it aloud to a friend. Ask your friend if it makes sense. Ask your friend to ask you a few questions. You may have forgotten to write something that is obvious to you but not to someone who reads or listens to the article. This will help you to improve the article. For example:

- Did you go to this place alone or with your family?
- Where is _____?
- How did you feel when you first arrived?

HINT
- Remember to describe the challenges you faced and the advantages of living in the place.
- Try to use interesting compound adjectives, relative clauses and quantifiers in your story.
- Remember to check your spelling!
- Look at the layout of the article that you read on page 148. Use the same or a similar layout. You can write by hand or on a computer.

CHALLENGE YOURSELF

Write another article in which you express a completely different opinion about staying in the same place. In other words, if your first article expresses a view that the experience was fun and exciting, your second article should express the view that it was not a good experience.

Self check
- Did you try to use a magazine layout for your article?
- Did you give special attention to the first paragraph?
- Did you include a picture or a photograph with a caption?
- Did you describe your feelings and opinions about the experience quite clearly?

What can you do?

Now you have completed Unit 9, you may like to try the Unit 9 online knowledge test if you are using the Boost eBook.

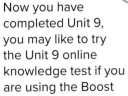

Read and review what you can do.
- I can listen to a programme about where movies are filmed.
- I can talk about visiting and living in remote places.
- I can listen to a podcast about how to survive in a remote place.
- I can read about film locations.
- I can read about the challenges of living in remote places.
- I can write an article about living in a remote place.
- I can use a range of different adjectives and quantifiers.
- I can use relative clauses.

Review Units 7–9

TRY THIS

Work in pairs and complete the conversation. Use the correct forms of the words in brackets.

Ken: Have you (hear) the news? There (to be) no exams this year! What joy!

Anna: That's fake news! I don't (belief) it!

Ken: I promise you. It's true.

Anna: What is your source of information?

Ken: I (reading) about it on social media.

Anna: But you (say) yesterday that that was not a reliable source?

Ken: Um … yes. Well … it would be quite an (interest) idea though, I mean …

Anna: Stop (dream), Ken. It's not (go) to happen!

Ken: I suppose you are right, as usual.

PRACTISE

Use words from the box to complete these sentences.

rugged	influenced	remote	**brand**	success
influencers	scams	location	distort	source

1 Our market stall was a great _____!
2 Do you follow any _____ on social media?
3 What do you think is the best _____ for news you can trust?
4 Fake news can _____ information and make people upset and confused.
5 Are you _____ by the news to believe something that may not be true?
6 The landscape on the island is quite _____.
7 A place that is far away from where most people live is a _____ place.
8 The TV series *Game of Thrones* was filmed on _____ in Croatia and Malta.
9 We need to be careful of internet _____ that try to get us to reveal our personal details.
10 Which _____ of shampoo do you use?

PRACTISE

Can you write these sentences correctly? You will need to choose the correct words to do this.

1 Surfing gives me so much (joy/joyful/joyous) that I would like to do it as my job one day. (Abstract nouns)
2 When (is going/will/shall) the actors be arriving? (Future forms)
3 Can we go (fish/fishing/fished) in the river this weekend? (Gerunds)
4 (Shake hands/Handshake/Handshaking) has been banned in our town. (Gerunds)
5 My friend (is telling/tell/told) us that we must fact-check what we read. (Reported speech)
6 Jo asked Ali (if he listened/he listening/if he listening) to the news on the radio. (Reported speech)
7 We took a (day five/five days/five-day) tour of New Zealand last year. (Compound adjectives)
8 Alya and Ken were very (excited/exciting/excite) about the trip. (Adjectives)
9 I have seen (a few/much/none) films that were filmed in London. (Quantifiers)
10 Do you know (why/who/which) they chose this location for the film? (Relative clauses)

LET'S TALK

Work in pairs. You have been asked to find a suitable location to shoot a film about a group of young people who go on a trip to a remote place. They will do several outdoor activities and one of them will get lost during the activities, or there will be a bad storm and the young people will be stranded and have to work out how to survive.

1 Look at the photographs and describe the landscape in each photograph.
2 Then discuss which place would be suitable for making the film. You will have to give reasons for your choice to the director of the film.

PRACTISE

1 In Unit 7 you wrote a business plan and took part in a market day at school. Now use the skills you have learned to write a report about the activity. Think about these questions:
  ● What were your goals?
  ● Did you achieve them?
  ● Did you make a profit?
  ● What did you learn from the experience?

2 Draft a short report of three paragraphs. You can use the following structure:
  ● Paragraph 1: Explain briefly what you did. Say where and when the market took place and what your stall sold.
  ● Paragraph 2: Provide some facts about what you achieved (for example, how much profit you made).
  ● Paragraph 3: Give your opinion about the plan and about the market day. What did you learn? What did you enjoy? Was this a successful activity or not?

You can publish your report on your school website or social media page or newspaper.

CHALLENGE YOURSELF

Work in pairs to write a magazine article in which you express an opinion about travel to remote parts of the world. Do you think it is good for the environment?

Grammar

Abstract nouns

Abstract nouns describe things that you cannot see or feel or touch, such as ideas and thoughts. For example:

- happiness, fun, achievement

Adjectives

Adjectives describe nouns and pronouns and allow us to make comparisons. For example:

- This is an <u>eerie</u> place!
- That is the <u>most beautiful</u> place I have ever visited.
- She is <u>taller</u> than her sister.

We can form adjectives with the suffixes -ing and -ed. For example:

- interested, interesting

Adjectives do not agree with the noun or pronoun they describe. They do not have plural forms.

Some adjectives have irregular comparative and superlative forms. For example:

- good, better, best

Adverbs

Adverbs modify (tell us more about) verbs, adjectives and other adverbs. Adverbs can be words or phrases. They describe manner, place and time.

You can use adverbs to compare actions. For example:

- high, higher, the highest

If an adverb has more than two syllables, you add 'more' or 'most' to make comparisons.

Adverbial phrases tell you more about a verb, just like adverbs do. They do not have a verb.

Compound adjectives

Compound adjectives consist of two words. We usually write these adjectives with a hyphen. For example:

- A five-hour trip.
- A second-hand book.

Compound nouns

Compound nouns consist of two nouns. For example:
- classroom, dishcloth

Conditional clauses

First conditional

We use the first conditional if there is a very real possibility that something will happen in the future. For example:
- If you arrive late, you will miss the train. (If + present simple tense + will)

Zero conditional clauses (with 'if')

We use the zero conditional to say things we know are true and to talk about science facts. For example:
- If you heat ice, it melts. (If + present simple = present simple)

Connectives

Connectives link words, clauses, sentences and ideas when we speak and when we write.

Connectives also help to put events in sequence. For example:
- before, after, then, while, when

We use connectives to give explanations, examples and reasons. For example:
- and, because, or, but, although, therefore, so, so that, such

Pronouns can also help to connect ideas because they refer back to nouns.

Gerunds

Gerunds are action nouns that look like verbs. We form gerunds by adding -ing to a verb stem.

A gerund can be the subject of a sentence. For example:
- Swimming is my passion!

In this sentence the gerund is before the verb.

A gerund can be the object of a sentence. For example:
- I have stopped reading the news, because so much of it is fake news!

In this sentence the gerund is after the verb in the main clause.

After some verbs we can use an infinitive or a gerund. For example:
- I love acting. I love to act.

The following verbs are always followed by a gerund: enjoy, keep, mind, finish, stop.

Infinitives

The infinitive form of a verb is a verb that has 'to' in front of it. For example:
- They want to surf this afternoon.

Modal verbs

Modal verbs are verbs that are added to the main verb to express permission, obligation, advice, possibility or ability. Modal verbs do not change form.

Use the infinitive without 'to' after modal verbs:
- can, could: possibility and ability
- may, might: possibility
- must, have to: obligation
- should: give advice, make suggestions
- must: necessity
- may, can: permission
- can, may: make requests
- can't: prohibition

Phrases

A phrase is a group of two or more words, without a verb. We can make noun, adjectival, adverbial and prepositional phrases.

Noun phrases

A noun phrase is a group of words (without a verb) that makes sense. You can replace the noun with a noun phrase. For example:
- People in the streets were queueing to buy the pizzas.

Prepositional phrases

We can use prepositions before adjectives and nouns in prepositional phrases.

Prepositional phrases start with prepositions. For example:
- She left on the fast train.

Dependent phrases

Some phrases depend on certain prepositions for their meanings. We always use these prepositions after certain adjectives or verbs to make phrases with a certain meaning. For example:
- I am happy with my choice.
- I couldn't do the crossword puzzle so I gave up.

Prepositions

Prepositions describe location, time and direction. For example:

- in, on, under, at, near, towards, off

Quantifiers

Quantifiers describe quantities. They tell us how many or how much there is of something. For example:

- all, some, any, no, less, few, most, both, plenty of, enough

Relative clauses and pronouns

Relative clauses are clauses that begin with relative pronouns such as who, that, which, whom, whose, where and why. These pronouns link the clauses.

We use 'who' to refer to people.

'Whom' is quite formal. Many people would use 'who' or 'that' instead of 'whom'.

Clauses can be defining or non-defining. You can remove a non-defining clause and the sentence will still make sense. For example:

- This is the house where she used to stay. (defining clause)
- Maria, who you met last week, is my best friend. (non-defining clause)

Reported and direct speech

Direct speech

We use this to quote the actual words that someone spoke. Direct speech is always inside speech marks (' and ').

Reported speech

We use reported speech to say what someone said. In reported speech we change the pronouns, the tense of the main verb, demonstratives and any adverbs of time. The word order changes too.

For example:

	Direct speech	Indirect speech
statement	'I have fish and chips,' said the woman.	The woman said she had fish and chips.
question	'Do you know this word?' the teacher asked.	The teacher asked if I knew that word.
command	'Bring your gym clothes tomorrow', the captain told us.	The captain told us to bring our gym clothes the next day.

Sentences

Sentences have:
- a subject (the person doing the action)
- a verb (the action).

Most sentences also need:
- an object (the thing the action happens to).

The subject and object of a sentence are usually nouns.

Verbs

Active and passive voices

We can use the active voice or the passive voice of verbs to describe present actions.

For example:

Active voice	Passive voice
They play baseball in summer.	Baseball is played in summer.
They made clothes in this factory last year.	Clothes were made in this factory last year.

To form the passive, use the verb 'to be' in different tenses + past participle.

Remember that some past participles are irregular. See the list on page 162.

Future forms

There are different future forms:

To describe plans and arrangements that have already been made. For example:
- We are going to visit friends this evening. (use going to + verb stem)

To make predictions. For example:
- The sport will appeal to young people.
- I shall be famous one day! (use will/shall + verb stem)

To describe future arrangements with fixed dates. For example:
- The new school year starts on 7 September. (use the present tense)

Past continuous tense

We use this tense to describe an action that was in progress while something else was happening. For example:
- As I was getting on the train, I dropped my phone.

To form this tense: verb 'to be' in the past form (was, were) + present participle (-ing).

Past simple tense

We usually form the simple past tense -ed. For example:
- play = played
- dance = danced

Some past tense verbs have irregular past tense forms. For example:
- go = went
- take = took

Look at the list of irregular past tense verbs on page 162 if you are not sure.

Present continuous tense

We use this tense to say what is happening at the moment, as we are speaking. For example:
- I am watching the other passengers on the train.

We also use this tense to talk about future arrangements. For example:
- We are going to Prague next month.

To form this tense: verb 'to be' (am, is, are) + present participle (-ing).

Present perfect tense

We use this tense to describe a recent or unfinished action that we did in the past and that we are still doing or hope to do in the future.

To form this tense use the verb 'have/has' + past participle.

Present simple tense

We use the present simple tense:
- to talk about habits and routines
- to describe people
- to talk about things that are always true.

For example:
- He/she wears school uniform.

The verb for the third person singular ends in -s.

Irregular verb forms

Infinitive	Present participle	Simple past	Past participle
to be	being	was/were	been
to beat	beating	beat	beaten
to become	becoming	became	become
to begin	beginning	began	begun
to bend	bending	bent	bent
to bite	biting	bit	bitten
to bleed	bleeding	bled	bled
to blow	blowing	blew	blown
to break	breaking	broke	broken
to bring	bringing	brought	brought
to build	building	built	built
to burn	burning	burnt, burned	burnt, burned
to buy	buying	bought	bought
to catch	catching	caught	caught
to choose	choosing	chose	chosen
to come	coming	came	come
to cut	cutting	cut	cut
to dig	digging	dug	dug
to draw	drawing	drew	drawn
to do	doing	did	done
to drink	drinking	drank	drunk
to drive	driving	drove	driven
to eat	eating	ate	eaten
to fall	falling	fell	fallen
to feel	feeling	felt	felt
to find	finding	found	found
to fly	flying	flew	flown
to forget	forgetting	forgotten	forgotten
to get	getting	got	got
to give	giving	gave	given
to go	going	went	gone
to grow	growing	grew	grown
to have	having	had	had
to hear	hearing	heard	heard
to hide	hiding	hid	hidden
to hit	hitting	hit	hit
to hold	holding	held	held
to hurt	hurting	hurt	hurt
to keep	keeping	kept	kept
to know	knowing	knew	known
to learn	learning	learned, learnt	learned, learnt

Infinitive	Present participle	Simple past	Past participle
to leave	leaving	left	left
to lend	lending	lent	lent
to let	letting	let	let
to lie	lying	lied	lied
to lie (down)	lying	lay	lain
to light	lighting	lit, lighted	lit, lighted
to lose	losing	lost	lost
to make	making	made	made
to mean	meaning	meant	meant
to meet	meeting	met	met
to pay	paying	paid	paid
to put	putting	put	put
to read	reading	read	read
to ride	riding	rode	ridden
to ring	ringing	rung	rung
to run	running	ran	run
to say	saying	said	said
to see	seeing	saw	seen
to sell	selling	sold	sold
to send	sending	sent	sent
to sew	sewing	sewed	sewn
to show	showing	showed	shown
to shut	shutting	shut	shut
to sing	singing	sang	sung
to sit	sitting	sat	sat
to sleep	sleeping	slept	slept
to slide	sliding	slid	slid
to smell	smelling	smelt, smelled	smelt, smelled
to speak	speaking	spoke	spoken
to spend	spending	spent	spent
to stand	standing	stood	stood
to steal	stealing	stole	stolen
to swim	swimming	swam	swum
to take	taking	took	taken
to teach	teaching	taught	taught
to tell	telling	told	told
to think	thinking	thought	thought
to throw	throwing	threw	thrown
to understand	understanding	understood	understood
to wake (up)	waking	woke	woken
to wear	wearing	wore	worn
to win	winning	won	won
to write	writing	wrote	written

Punctuation

A B C	Capital letters are used for the first letter of a name, country, place, nationality, days of the week, months of the year or language.
.	A full stop shows the end of a sentence. It may also be used after initials, e.g. N.J. Hill and abbreviations, e.g. B.B.C.
,	A comma shows a short pause that separates parts of a sentence or words in a list.
( )	Brackets show extra information or an explanation which is considered less important.
" " or ' '	Speech marks show words that are spoken directly. They are also used around the title of films and books. Speech marks may be double – " " or single – ' '.
'	An apostrophe is used when two words are contracted. It is also used to show possession, e.g. it's Bill's.
-	A hyphen is used when two words such as compound nouns are joined together, e.g. son-in-law.
?	A question mark is used at the end of a sentence which asks a direct question. It is also used for requests. Can you buy some milk, please?
:	A colon is used to show that something is coming next, e.g. a list.

Glossary

achievement (noun) something you have succeeded in doing, with some effort

apartheid (noun) a political system which separated people according to their race and which did not allow people their full rights

appeal (noun) a serious or strong request

appeal (verb) to make a serious request, or when something or someone is seen as attractive or interesting

attract (verb) to make someone like something

avatar (noun) a figure which represents someone (on the internet, in a game)

biotechnology (noun) the use of living organisms to make products

brand (noun) name of a product used to sell the product

bravery (noun) behaviour which shows courage in dangerous situations

bullet (noun) small piece of metal which shoots out of a gun

bump (verb) to knock or hit against something hard

bump (noun) a knock or hit against something hard

bumpy (adjective) not flat or smooth

campaign (noun) organised activities which have a particular aim

campaign (verb) to take part in organised activities with a particular aim

cancel (verb) to stop a planned activity

cargo (noun) goods that are transported

carriage (noun) a section of a train in which people sit

catfishing (noun) stealing someone's profile or setting up fake profiles to lure people into starting online relationships

ceremony (noun) a formal public or religious event

chase (verb) to follow and try to catch someone or something

chat (verb) to talk (informal)

chat (noun) an informal conversation, especially online and on social media

class (noun) a group of people who are the same in some way

climate change (noun) a permanent change in weather conditions

coincidence (noun) not connected but happening at the same time or place by chance

community (noun) a group of people who live in the same place or according to the same ideas

compromise (noun) an agreement in which people get part of what they want

concern (noun) something that is important or interesting and which somebody cares about

confetti (noun) small pieces of paper (or rice or flowers) that are thrown during a ceremony

co-ordination (noun) organising things so that they work together

costume (noun) a set of clothes particular to a certain country, activity, or period of history. May be worn to look like someone else (e.g. for a party)

courage (noun) bravery

dear (adjective) special and loved

dependable (adjective) can be trusted, reliable

development (noun) getting bigger, growth

digital (adjective) operating electronically

diligent (adjective) taking care to do work properly and completely

direct (adjective) straight

direct (verb) to control or manage

disciplined (adjective) following the rules, in a controlled way

disembark (verb) to get off a ship, boat, train or aeroplane

disinformation (noun) false information

distort (verb) change the shape or meaning of something

earnest (adjective) keen, serious

easy-going (adjective) relaxed, informal

eco-friendly (adjective) not harming the environment

effort (noun) energy used to do something

encourage (verb) to give support or hope to

encouraging (adjective) giving hope

enterprise (noun) a business or plan

entrepreneur (noun) a person who sets up a business in order to make money

environment (noun) everything around us

event (noun) something that happens

extraordinary (adjective) very special and unusual

extreme (adjective) very strong, far or great

fabulous (adjective) very nice or good

fact-check (verb) check if something is true

fantastic (adjective) wonderful, very good

film crew (noun) group of people who make films

film set (noun) place where film is made or filmed

fireworks (noun) something that explodes and makes colours and patterns when you light it

flagpole (noun) a pole on which a flag hangs or flies

forgiving (adjective) willing to stop being angry about something someone did

frozen (adjective) made hard by cold temperature, stopped moving

funny (adjective) humorous, makes you laugh

gender (noun) being female or male

handlebars (noun) part of bicycle which you hold with your hands

headline (noun) the title of an article in a newspaper or magazine, in big letters

hoop (noun) a big ring of metal, wood or plastic

impact (noun) the effect of something

impatiently (adverb) showing you are annoyed because you cannot wait for something

important (adjective) something of value or that affects many people and things

impressive (adjective) something that can be admired

in common (adjective) shared interest, experience or characteristic

inclusivity (noun) being included or part of a group

industry (noun) business, economic activity in which goods are made

influence (noun) the power to change things

influencer (noun) a person who gets others to do or buy things

informal (adjective) relaxed, friendly

innovation (noun) new way of doing something

interest (noun) wanting to be involved with or know more about something

interesting (adjective) something you enjoy or want to know more about

island (noun) land with water around it

journey (noun) a trip to or from a place

landfill (noun) place where waste material is buried

landscape (noun) an area of land that you can see

lie (noun) something said that is not true

lie (verb) to say something that is not true

lie (verb) to put body in horizontal position or flat on a surface

location (noun) place

logo (noun) symbol or picture that represents a product or business

manipulate (verb) to change something so that it is to your own advantage

media (noun, plural) ways of communicating that reach large numbers of people, such as newspapers, magazines, television, radio and the internet

medium (noun) a means or tool to do something; a way of communicating to a large number of people

misinformation (noun) information that is not correct or true

mute (verb) to turn down the volume of something until there is no sound

nearby (preposition) something that is close in distance; not too far away

needed (verb past participle; adjective) to have a requirement or a need for something

negotiate (verb) to bargain with someone in order to reach an agreement

nice (adjective) something or someone that is good, pleasant, agreeable and/or kind

non-judgemental (adjective) someone who does not form bad or disapproving opinions of others

noodles (noun) flat, narrow strips of dough that have been dried and then boiled to make them soft for eating

nutrients (noun) nutrients are found in food and help plants and animals live and grow

online (adjective) connected to or reached through a computer network

opinion (noun) what someone thinks of somebody or something, usually based on facts, feelings or experiences

opposition (noun) being against someone or something

outcast (noun) a person who has been rejected by their social group or by society

parade (noun) a public procession of people, marching bands, or vehicles in front of spectators as part of a celebration or ceremony

parade (verb) to walk about or proceed in front of a person or people

participate (verb) to take part or share in something

patiently (adverb) waiting without becoming upset or angry

phishing (verb/gerund) pronounced 'fishing', phishing are emails or text messages sent by criminals trying to obtain personal details such as passwords and bank details. The messages may look like they are from a trustworthy source to try and fool the reader

plait (noun) strands of hair, or cloth, that have been woven together in a braid

platform (noun) raised surface used as a place to stand, or as a stage

platform (noun) a space for shared content and ideas, often online

pollution (noun) poisons, wastes or other items that are being thrown away into nature without regard for the damage they cause

post (verb) putting something, such as a photograph, on an online platform for others to see

postpone (verb) to put off something until later

private messaging (noun phrase) to send someone a message on an online platform that only they can see

proposition (noun) an idea or opinion, that is offered to others so that it can be discussed

prosthetic (noun) an artificial limb

race (noun) a competition of speed, for example a running race

race (noun) a human population sharing certain common physical characteristics that have been passed down from one generation to the next

race (verb) to take part in a competition of speed

real (adjective) something that is not imaginary, that actually exists or is true

recycle (verb) to put things through a process so that they can be reused

reflect (verb) to think about something

reject (verb) to refuse to take, believe or approve of something

reliable (adjective) something that you can trust, or on which you can depend

religion (noun) a set of beliefs about how the universe was made and what its purpose is

remote (adjective) far away from something

research (verb) to study something carefully in order to find out information about it

respectful (adjective) to be polite and show regard for others

rugged (adjective) having a surface which is rough, uneven or rocky

rumour (noun) a piece of information that is not proven by fact, which is spread through conversation

scam (noun) a dishonest plan or operation which cheats people

sculpture (noun) the art of making statues or other objects which have been chiselled, moulded or carved

security (noun) something that protects you

segregation (noun) the practice of separating people into groups, often racial groups

severe (adjective) something that is very strict, harsh or strong

shelter (noun) a place that protects you from bad weather or danger

shrine (noun) a sacred place that honours an important person or god

sincere (adjective) something that is genuine, not fake or pretend

skins (noun) a bonus feature in a video game that allows your character to change appearance

social media (noun phrase) online platforms, like websites and apps, that allow people to share information and photographs, and communicate with one another

software (noun) any programs written to operate a computer or other machine

solar-powered (adjective) something that is powered using energy from the sun

source (noun) the start or cause of something

special (adjective) something that is not ordinary, or something that is better than normal

startup (noun) a new company started by an entrepreneur

steam (noun) water vapour that is released into the air by heated water

steep (adjective) something that is on a sharp slope or slant

studio (noun) a place where an artist works, or a special room or building in which films, music, radio, or television shows are produced or broadcast

success (noun) a person or thing that does well, or achieves an intended goal

supportive (adjective) something or someone that provides assistance, help or encouragement

suspicious (adjective) someone or something that causes questions or doubt, which cannot be trusted

sweet (adjective) something that is pleasant, or something with a sweet taste such as sugar or honey

sweet (noun) something with a sweet taste, such as cookies or candy

technology (noun) inventions and methods of solving problems that come out of research

time zones (noun phrase) regions in which all the clocks are set to the same time. Time zones differ depending on where you are

tough (adjective) something that is difficult to deal with; something or someone that is strong

trails (noun) pathways through nature, for example, over mountains

tricks (noun) something done to fool or cheat someone, or an act of skill or magic

underground (adjective) something that is below the surface of the earth; hidden from the public

underground (noun) a place below the earth's surface

vague (adjective) something that is not clear, or difficult to understand

waste (noun) items that are not useful anymore and are thrown away, like trash

waste (verb) to use or spend something in a careless way, or to not take full advantage of something

waves (noun) a moving swell on a surface of water

web cam (noun) abbreviation for World Wide Web Camera, a camera designed to take photographs, videos or live streams, and put them onto internet platforms

website (noun) a location on the internet or world wide web where information may be shared

zero-waste (adjective) a way of living in which you try to damage the planet as little as possible, by reducing your waste, re-using items and recycling items

Pronunciation words

A

Adam

Ali

Alice

Alton

Alya

Amelia

American

Amina

Amsterdam

Andy

Anief

Anne

apartheid

Australia

B

baobab tree

Basingstoke

basket

Bella

Ben

Bill Gates

Billie Eilish

biotechnology

Birmingham

bizarre

Boomslang

Brazil

bruises

Bulgaria

C

California

Cameron Herold

campaign

Canada

cancel

Cape Town

carriage

Chad le Clos

Chadwick Boseman

chef

China

communicate

compromise

confetti

Copacabana beach

corridor

courage

cousin

criteria

D

Daniel

DanTDM

Darren

David

debate

dependable

dictating

Dubai

Dylan

E

eco-friendly

Egypt

Elizabeth

Elon Musk

engineering

entrepreneurs

environment

Europe

extraordinary

F

fabulous

Farah

Florida

France

G

Germany

germs

Gothenburg

Greece

Greta Thunberg

H

Hawaii

hazardous

Hong Kong

household

I

Iceland

India

Italy

J

Japan

Jasmine

John

Jon

Jose

José Alberto Pujols Alcántara

K

Ken

King Abdullah

Kirstenbosch Gardens

knit

knock

L

landfill

Lara

Laszlo Cseh

Le Metro

Lebohang

Lee

lemurs

licence

Luc

M

Madagascar

Majora Carter

Malala Yousafzai

Malaysia

Malik

Malta

Mano

Mara

Maria

Marik

Mark

Mary

mask

May

Maya Penn

medieval

Meera

Mexico

Michael Phelps

Mika

Milo

mime

minstrels

modules

Mount Vesuvius

Mumbai

N

Nadir

Nairobi

Naples

Neeria

Nirmalya Kumar

Norway

nutritious

O

Oaxaca

P

Pakistan

Paris

passion

Paul Theroux

Paulo

persuade

Pete

polluting

psyched

pylons

R

Ramadan

Rami

recycling

referee

refugees

Robert Louis Stevenson

Rome

Rosa

rough

Russia

S

Sabine

Saira

Salma

Sanjay

Sarah

schedule

science

Scotland

sculpture

segregation

Simon Sinek

Singapore

South Korea

spreads

suburban

Sweden

T

Taekwondo

tattered

The Netherlands

timetables

traditional

Turkey

Tyrone

U

Uganda

United Kingdom

V

vague

Veerabhadra Temple

W

Waterloo Station

Woking

wrappers

Y

Yusei Kikuchi

Reading for enjoyment

Do you want to find out more about some of the topics you have learned about? Reading a range of fiction and non-fiction books for enjoyment will help build up your vocabulary in English. Use a dictionary to look up some words you don't know, but remember you don't have to look up every word you're not sure about because you can try and work it out from the context. It's a good idea to keep a reading journal, so you can record what you have read and what you thought about the book.

Here are some suggested fiction and non-fiction books you might like to try.

Third-party resources referred to in this section have not been endorsed by Cambridge Assessment International Education.

Winterborne Home for Vengeance and Valour (ISBN: 9781408357378)
by Ally Carter,
Orchard Books

Planet Omar: Accidental Trouble Magnet (ISBN: 9781444951226)
by Zanib Mian,
Hodder Children's Books

Deadfall: Book 3 (The Haven) (ISBN: 9781444947649)
by Simon Lelic,
Hodder Children's Books

My Awesome Guide to Getting Good at Stuff (ISBN: 9781526362681)
by Matthew Syed,
Wren & Rook

Go Big: The Secondary School Survival Guide (ISBN: : 9781526362353)
by Matthew Burton,
Wren & Rook

Women in Art: 50 Fearless Creatives Who Inspired the World (ISBN: 9781526362452)
by Rachel Ignotofsky,
Wren & Rook

Toto the Ninja Cat and the Great Snake Escape (ISBN: 9781444939453)
by Dermot O'Leary,
Hodder Children's Books

The Paper & Hearts Society Book 1: Find Your People (ISBN: 9781444949247)
by Lucy Powrie,
Hodder Children's Books

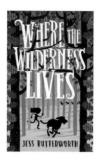

Where the Wilderness Lives
(ISBN: 9781510105508)
by Jess Butterworth,
Orion Children's Books

This Book Will (Help) Cool the Climate (ISBN: 9781526362414)
by Isabel Thomas,
Wren & Rook

Fire Boy (ISBN: 9781444954685)
by J M Joseph,
Hodder Children's Books

Boot: Small Robot, Big Adventure
(ISBN: 9781444949360)
by Shane Hegarty,
Hodder Children's Books

The Tail of Emily Windsnap
(ISBN: 9781444015096)
by Liz Kessler,
Orion Children's Books

Secrets in the Skies
(ISBN: 9781526360014)
by Giles Sparrow,
Wren & Rook

Find Your Girl Squad
(ISBN: 9781526362506)
by Dr Angharad Rudkin and
Ruth Fitzgerald,
Wren & Rook

Engineering Power! Machines in Space (ISBN: 9781526311801)
by Kay Barnham,
Wayland

The Boy at the Back of the Class
(ISBN: 9781510105010)
by Onjali Q Rauf,
Orion Children's Books

Stand Against: Prejudice
(ISBN: 9781445168210)
by Izzi Howell,
Franklin Watts

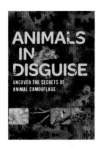

Animals in Disguise
(ISBN: 9781526312143)
by Michael Bright,
Wayland

*Space Science: STEM in Space:
Science for Rocketing into Space*
(ISBN: 9781526308115)
by Mark Thompson,
Wayland

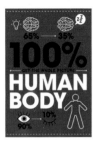

*100% Get the Whole Picture: Human
Body* (ISBN: 9781526308139)
by Paul Mason,
Wayland

*Space Science: STEM in Space:
Science for Exploring Outer Space*
(ISBN: 9781526308467)
by Mark Thompson,
Wayland

*Stand Against: Poverty and
Hunger* (ISBN: 9781445167398)
by Alice Harman,
Franklin Watts

Cats React to Science Facts
(ISBN: 9781526311160)
by Izzi Howell,
Scholastic Inc.

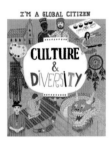

*I'm a Global Citizen: Culture and
Diversity* (ISBN: 9781445163987)
by Georgia Amson-Bradshaw,
Franklin Watts

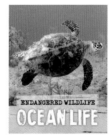

Endangered Wildlife: Ocean Life
(ISBN: 9781526310002)
by Anita Ganeri,
Wayland

Acknowledgements

Every effort has been made to trace all copyright holders, but if any have been inadvertently overlooked, the Publishers will be pleased to make the necessary arrangements at the first opportunity.

Text credits

p.50 Courtesy of Arab News; **p.78** Online and mobile safety, NSPCC, Used with permission. Retrieved from https://www.childline.org.uk/info-advice/bullying-abuse-safety/online-mobile-safety/; **p.118** Todd Prodanovich.

Image credits

r = right, *l* = left, *b* = bottom, *t* = top, *m* = middle

p.6 *l* © Goodluz/stock.adobe.com; *r* © Lightfield Studios/stock.adobe.com; **p.8** © Asier/stock.adobe.com; **p.9** *t* © Torgado/Shutterstock.com; *b* © Adzicnatasa/stock.adobe.com; **p.11** © Svetography/stock.adobe.com; **p.12** *t* © New Africa/stock.adobe.com; *b* © Stocker1970/Shutterstock.com; **p.13** © Pololia/stock.adobe.com; **p.14–15** © Lisa F. Young/stock.adobe.com; **p.15** *b* © Highwaystarz/stock.adobe.com; **p.16** *l* © Diego cervo/stock.adobe.com; *r* © Africa Studio/stock.adobe.com; **p.17** *l* © Masson/stock.adobe.com; *r* © Iyd39/Shutterstock.com; **p.19** © BillionPhotos.com/stock.adobe.com; **p.22** *t l* © Roberto Sorin/Shutterstock.com; *t r* © Dina Saeed/Shutterstock.com; *b l* © Creativa Images/Shutterstock.com; *b r* © Mark Fisher/Shutterstock.com; **p.23** © Rogerio Cavalheiro/Shutterstock.com; **p.24** © Scalia Media/stock.adobe.com; **p.25** *l* © Mikhail mandrygin/123 RF.com; *r* © Iakov Filimonov/Shutterstock.com; **p.26** *l* © Achiaos/Shutterstock.com; *r* © Ferrari Septiano/Shutterstock.com; **p.28** *t* © ComposedPix/Shutterstock.com; *m* © Africa Studio/stock.adobe.com; *r* © Just Another Photographer/Shutterstock.com; **p.30** © Jag_cz/stock.adobe.com; **p.31** © Phive2015/stock.adobe.com; **p.32** *l* © AppleEyesStudio/Shutterstock.com; *r* © Oatawa/stock.adobe.com; **p.33** *t* © Gary Hershorn/Shutterstock.com; *m* © Pajor Pawel/Shutterstock.com; *b* © Photocarioca/Shutterstock.com; **p.34** © TEEREXZ/stock.adobe.com; **p.36** © Grobler du Preez/123 RF.com; **p.38** *t l* © Imray/stock.adobe.com; *t r* © Kanvag/stock.adobe.com; *b l* © Airborne77/stock.adobe.com; *b r* © Roman Milert/stock.adobe.com; **p.42** *l* © Foton1601/stock.adobe.com; *r* © Perytskyy/stock.adobe.com; **p.43** © Curto/stock.adobe.com; **p.44** © Richard Carey/stock.adobe.com; **p.46** © Arnaudmartinez/stock.adobe.com; **p.47** © Surawutob/Shutterstock.com; **p.48** © Pixel-Shot/stock.adobe.com; **p.50** Courtesy of Arab News; **p.51** © Tashanatasha/stock.adobe.com; **p.52** *t l* © Apolinarias/Shutterstock.com; *t r* © Sunethrt/Shutterstock.com; *b l* © Zsuzsanna/stock.adobe.com; *b r* © M.malinika/stock.adobe.com; **p.55** *l* © Pixel-Shot/stock.adobe.com; *r* © Roberto Sorin/Shutterstock.com; **p.56** *t l* © Aleksei/stock.adobe.com; *t m* © Scanrail/stock.adobe.com; *t r* © Kev Gregory/Shutterstock.com; *b l* © Goran Bogicevic/Shutterstock.com; *b m* © Scaliger/stock.adobe.com; *b r* © Fabio Lamanna/Shutterstock.com; **p.58** *t* © Rawpixel.com/stock.adobe.com; *b* © Paul Nicholas UK/Shutterstock.com; **p.59** © Phpetrunina14/stock.adobe.com; **p.61** *t l* © Ryan_Cheng/stock.adobe.com; *t r* © Pongpinun/stock.adobe.com; *b l* © F11photo/stock.adobe.com; *b r* © C623/stock.adobe.com; **p.62** *t* © Yali Shi/stock.adobe.com; *b* © Daboost/stock.adobe.com; **p.64** © Daboost/stock.adobe.com; **p.65** © Faboi/Shutterstock.com; **p.66** © Klublu/Shutterstock.com; **p.68** *t l* © M Selcuk Oner/Shutterstock.com; *t r* © Shutterstock.com; *b l* © JFL Photography/stock.adobe.com; *b r* © Mazur Travel/stock.adobe.com; **p.69** © Vencav/stock.adobe.com; **p.70** © Den-belitsky/stock.adobe.com; **p.72** *l* © Highwaystarz/stock.adobe.com; *r* © Alphaspirit/stock.adobe.com; **p.73** © Sascha Burkard/stock.adobe.com; **p.74** © John Blanton/Shutterstock.com; **p.75** *t l* © Syda Productions/stock.adobe.com; *t r* © Syda Productions/stock.adobe.com; *b l* © Ljupco Smokovski/stock.adobe.com; *b r* © Gezzeg/stock.adobe.com; **p.76** © Sdecoret/stock.adobe.com; **p.81** *t* © Natalia/stock.adobe.com; *b* © Nina design/Shutterstock.com; **p.84** ©

Gorodenkoff/stock.adobe.com; **p.85** © Gorodenkoff/stock.adobe.com; **p.88** *t l* © Yanik88/stock.adobe.com; *t m* © Noraisman Sahran/123 RF.com; *t r* © Emran/Shutterstock.com; *m l* © Witthaya/stock.adobe.com; *m r* © EvrenKalinbacak/Shutterstock.com; *b l* © Jorge A. Russell/Shutterstock.com; *b m* © Graham Hunt/ProSports/Shutterstock.com; *b r* © Mai Groves/Shutterstock.com; **p.90** © EvrenKalinbacak/Shutterstock.com; *r* © Jorge A. Russell/Shutterstock.com; **p.91** © The European Powerchair Football Association/Fédération Internationale de Powerchair Football Association *r* © Leremy/stock.adobe.com; **p.92** © Izf/stock.adobe.com; **p.93** © Georgy Dzyura/stock.adobe.com; **p.94** *l* © Kuremo/Shutterstock.com; *r* © Fxquadro/stock.adobe.com; **p.95** © Fxquadro/stock.adobe.com; **p.96** © Photocreo Bednarek/stock.adobe.com; **p.98** © Pressmaster/stock.adobe.com; **p.99** © Yevheniy Kornyeyev/stock.adobe.com; **p.100** *t* © Keeton Gale/Shutterstock.com; *b* © Nippon News/Aflo Co. Ltd./Alamy Live News/Alamy Stock Photo; **p.101** © Andrey Popov/stock.adobe.com; **p.102** © Chong Voon Chung/Xinhua/Alamy Live News/Alamy Stock Photo; **p.103** © Chong Voon Chung/Xinhua/Alamy Live News/Alamy Stock Photo; **p.104** © Sergey/stock.adobe.com; **p.105** © Acres/stock.adobe.com; **p.106** *l* © Dpa picture alliance/Alamy Stock Photo; *r* © Billy Bennight/AdMedia via ZUMA Press, Inc./Alamy Stock Photo; **p.107** *l* © Jasper Chamber/Alamy Stock Photo; *r* © Richard Goldschmidt/Alamy Live News/Alamy Stock Photo; **p.108** *l* © Joe Marino/Bill Cantrell-UPI/Alamy Stock Photo; *r* © Cheese Scientist/Alamy Stock Photo; **p.110** © Dpa picture alliance/Alamy Stock Photo; **p.111** *t* © Jasper Chamber/Alamy Stock Photo; *b* © Picture Capital/Alamy Live News/Alamy Stock Photo; **p.114** © Nancy Kaszerman/ZUMA Press, Inc./Alamy Live News/Alamy Stock Photo; **p.115** © Picture Capital/Alamy Live News; **p.118** © Amy Sanderson/ZUMA Press, Inc./Alamy Live News/Alamy Stock Photo; **p.119** © Satit sewtiw/Shutterstock.com; **p.122** *t l* © MclittleStock/stock.adobe.com; *t r* © Scanrail/stock.adobe.com; *b l* © M-SUR/stock.adobe.com; *b r* © Rawpixel.com/stock.adobe.com; **p.124** *l* © Monster Ztudio/stock.adobe.com; *r* © Vchalup/stock.adobe.com; **p.125** *t* © VadimGuzhva/stock.adobe.com; *b* © Jeff Bukowski/stock.adobe.com; **p.128** © Onephoto/stock.adobe.com; **p.130** © WavebreakMediaMicro/stock.adobe.com; **p.131** © WavebreakMediaMicro/stock.adobe.com; **p.132** © 2207918/stock.adobe.com; **p.133** © Africa Studio/stock.adobe.com; **p.134** © Syda Productions/stock.adobe.com; **p.135** © Nata_vkusidey/stock.adobe.com; **p.138** *t l* © Ead72/stock.adobe.com; *t r* © Sagar Budha/Shutterstock.com; *b l* © Malajscy/stock.adobe.com; *b r* © Phungatanee/Shutterstock.com; **p.140** *t l* © GuruXOX/stock.adobe.com; *t r* © Cineberg/Shutterstock.com; *m* © Nghia Khanh/Shutterstock.com; *b l* © 1000Photography/Shutterstock.com; *b r* © Phant/stock.adobe.com; **p.142** © Phant/stock.adobe.com; **p.144** *t* © Michaklootwijk/stock.adobe.com; *m* © Vaclav/stock.adobe.com; *b* © Jon Anders Wiken/stock.adobe.com; **p.145** © Evekka/Shutterstock.com; **p.146** © Irisphoto1/stock.adobe.com; **p.147** © Irisphoto1/stock.adobe.com; **p.148** © Josep Suria/Shutterstock.com; **p.149** © Josep Suria//Shutterstock.com; **p.150** © Jacob Lund/stock.adobe.com; **p.152** *t* © Sinn P. Photography/Shutterstock.com; *b l* © Fotos593/Shutterstock.com; *b r* © Piotr Gatlik/Shutterstock.com; **p.155** *l* © Lim Yan Shan/Shutterstock.com; *r* © Hain.tarmann/Shutterstock.com